Great Beginnings for Music Teachers:

Mentoring and Supporting New Teachers

D1572946

Edited by Colleen M. Conway

Great Beginnings for Music Teachers:

Mentoring and Supporting New Teachers

The National Association for Music Education

Production Editor: Lisa Renfro

Copyright © 2003
MENC: The National Association for Music Education
1806 Robert Fulton Drive
Reston, VA 20191

Printed in the United States of America.
ISBN 1-56545-159-7

Contents

Foreword

Webster's definition of "mentor" ("a wise and trusted counselor or friend") is a disarmingly simple description of a unique developmental stage in the teacher induction process, a complex interplay between experience and inexperience, wisdom and naiveté, a stage of learning and intellectual development not included but clearly belonging in Bloom's Taxonomy. Effective mentoring prepares us for greater personal and professional leadership and success. It is an essential part of the development of the music education profession.

Mentoring goes far beyond the instinctual, habitual, repetitive, reinforcement, or pedagogical steps that comprise training. It is the sum of all of these steps. A high-order communication and learning process, mentoring is built on the analysis of professional-environment experiences, a learning cycle that includes observing, analyzing, and comparing known experiences and situations and applying them in new situations. Mentoring is not a short-term or once-in-a-while activity; its value grows because mentoring helps to develop an individual's experience, knowledge, and, eventually, wisdom. What sets mentoring apart from other activities is learning how to synthesize and apply knowledge to new situations. Done well, mentoring nurtures a reflective behavior in teaching that is essential to the growth of this art.

Great Beginnings for Music Teachers: Mentoring and Supporting New Teachers provides a significant milestone in the development of mentoring and induction in the music education profession. The characteristics of mentoring that I list above are thoroughly and articulately discussed by music educators who have carved out significant experiences important to the profession. The first real research- and experience-based contribution to understanding this process in music education, this book is a clarion call for new leaders in teacher induction programs.

I graduated from a large, distinguished school of music in a major Midwestern research university, but my first job was in a very different place—a small, charming, but provincial mill town on the banks of the Hudson River in upstate New York. This community had a history of hiring teachers from my university, and the placement office considered this position a "plum." While the community and district were very supportive during the interview, the real job, like those of most first-year teachers, was hardly a plum at first sight. The retiring band director had long ago given up on both music and disciplinary standards. The library and instrument inventories were a disaster. Yet my extensive interviews and the many rehearsals that I conducted with various student groups revealed the various layers of community interest and student ability that led me to believe that this could be a great first position.

From the outset I was the "new teacher from out west," and I found that everyone knew more about me than I knew about myself. The loss of anonymity was intrusive but curiously humorous. My accent *was* different, and my experiences in life had given me a different set of cultural, social, political, and educational expectations than the locals. Yet I knew that getting acclimatized was a part of teaching in a new community. I arrived in early August and worked virtually alone in the building, cataloging the library, cleaning the offices and rehearsal rooms, and planning the fall's activities.

The superintendent who had hired me and his wife asked me over for a porch supper one hot August evening. When I mentioned the obvious differences that I felt, the superintendent's response was quick and candid. "This is precisely the reason we hired you. Your background, experience, and expectations are what this community—and these young people—need. Go and do your work with our confidence, but take the time to know these good people and what they want for their children." My first experience with mentoring had begun, and I quickly realized that I needed help in understanding the community if I was to be successful.

The superintendent remained a valuable mentor, and those impromptu dinners became an important part of my first years. My landlord, Scott, a social studies teacher at the high school, helped me understand the dense network of relationships that extended between teachers, students, and the families of the community. The town had been founded by twelve families in 1792, and those families had multiplied many times. About half of the families in the town were related to each other, and the other half had been married to and divorced from the first half. Bruce, the art teacher, shared morning coffee with me and was a close friend and confidant from the first day. He shared the various political and social structures in the school district and community, and our mutual interests in music, art, and contemporary American culture led to the successful pursuit of a major grant in the interdisciplinary arts and an invaluable team-teaching relationship. His wife introduced me to her father, the town physician and a school board member. This sage old gentleman wanted the best for the students of the community. We spent many evenings talking about music and education and what needed to happen in this particular district. An older band director in a larger neighboring community helped me understand the complex contest system. We soon began visiting each other's rehearsals, and our lengthy discussions about our jobs, music teaching, repertoire selection, and instrument pedagogy were invaluable in my early professional development.

Why was this experience so positive? First, I wanted to learn and be helped. Second, these people wanted to help me; they cared about their school and community. Third, we developed a mutual trust based on mutual interest in our jobs, music, and teaching. Fourth, we did this together because we wanted to, not because we had to. There was no formal program, no district requirement, no extra pay. This mentoring process was beneficial because it was natural and authentic, not mandated, but desired and appreciated.

As I moved on to larger and more complex jobs, a dense network of mentor relationships—superiors and friends, superintendents and bank presidents, community leaders and foundation executives, teachers and parents, colleagues in other departments or civic boards—has provided an invaluable link between experience and learning, progress and success. I continue to go to these mentors all the time. Time and distance are of no concern in a real mentoring relationship; true mentors are those whom you can call upon at any time in your career.

The point of this story is that mentoring can come in several different varieties. Novice teachers need to have multiple mentors—some who can help with pedagogical or process issues; others who help to understand educational context, school climate, and environmental issues; and still others who offer a grounding in social or values issues. It is a rare person who can mentor in every area, and having only a single mentoring viewpoint may not be in everyone's best interest. How one accepts the information that mentors provide may depend on personality; different personalities provide different perspectives. Those of us who have invested in mentoring relationship as either mentors or mentees know that this is a long-term process, a continuum that contributes to career development. As experience accumulates and wisdom grows, the relationship becomes more fluid, elastic, and reciprocal. There is no proprietary role in mentoring. Since teaching is a highly plagiaristic yet individualized art, taking the best ideas, techniques, processes, and habits that you might learn from your mentor and applying them in new situations is a form of pedagogical flattery that validates the methodology that is part of mentoring.

Formal mentoring programs have been popular since the teacher profession-alism and accountability movement began in the mid-1980s, and this book is a sign that the music education profession is moving forward. And we need to.

We are faced with two critical problems: (1) an insufficient number of new music teachers to meet the national demand, and (2) an alarmingly high dropout rate among music teachers during their first five years of teaching. Only about 3,800 new music teachers graduate for the 11,000 vacancies that occur each year, and not all graduates actually teach. While the number of new music teachers is slowly increasing each year, it scarcely fills the gap between supply and demand, especially with the large pool of baby-boomer teachers nearing retirement. One way of relieving the pressure is to encourage more teachers to stay in the profession. Mentoring provides a network of relationships that can help those who enter the profession remain in the profession.

Bold state and national leadership is required to fully focus our attention on mentoring and induction. Mentoring is an important new investment opportunity for the professions's human and financial resources, perhaps even as vital to the future quality and quantity of teachers as the formulation of the National Standards was to curricular and programmatic accountability. If we spent only half the time and money on mentoring and induction that we spent on National Standards, we might really be able to make a difference. After all, without high-quality teachers teaching to the Standards, a significant opportunity to tie teaching quality to curricular accountability is lost.

What might this bold leadership in a systemic program of mentoring and induction look like? It will demand a new role for and the active engagement of state and national music education professional organizations, working hand in hand with K–12 districts and college and university music education programs. Mentoring and induction are not isolated events; they are important parts of a national strategy of teacher recruiting, preparation, induction, and professional development.

The authors of the chapters in this book cite specific examples and describe specific models in mentoring and induction that come from a rich collection of personal and professional experiences in music education. Their efforts are the blueprint for a national strategy. Many chapters provide links to the rich resources that exist in mentoring and induction programs in other fields of education and business. Some may feel that mentoring and induction activities are "new" and that we have to reinvent the wheel by starting this process from scratch. This book is ample proof that a significant body of experience for music education already exists.

I think that this book also demands that we develop a culture around mentoring that will require some significant changes in what importance we place on induction systems in our profession. This will require special conferences and symposia to raise the conversation about mentoring and induction. It will require a new relationship between prospective music educators, college music education students, and the profession. It will require action at many levels—not talk.

The point is, mentoring will never become a habit of mind and part of our culture of professional preparation until the profession *chooses* to make it so. Leadership means that we deliberately model the culture of mentoring throughout the teacher education process.

While I have great dreams that our state and national professional organizations, school districts, and college music programs will take the leadership role in developing mentoring and induction programs, ultimately it will be *individuals* who breathe life into these ideas, develop the models, engage partners around pilot programs, and create the impetus so critical for the efforts of our professional organizations. *Great Beginnings for Music Teachers: Mentoring and Supporting New Teachers* is *the* blueprint for this profession to use in seriously considering the role of mentoring and induction programs in retaining and keeping a new generation of music educators—and music *teacher* educators. We should heed its advice and study the models, for without doing so, we may indeed become a profession at risk.

—Jeffrey Kimpton, professor of
music education and director of the
School of Music at the University
of Minnesota–Minneapolis

A Career as a Music Teacher

Colleen M. Conway

> Being a music teacher is a lot of work and takes a lot of time; however, I can't think of a more worthwhile or meaningful career to have. The most rewarding aspect of the job is knowing that you can make a difference in the life of a child/person. I can still remember my first year of teaching and an experience I had during my sixth-grade band class. One day we were nearing the end of class and were playing through a full band piece for one of the first times. We finished the song, and while I'm assessing/evaluating the progress of the group in my own mind, thinking about all the things we need to do as a band to reach proficient performance, one of the flute players sitting in the front row looks up at me and says: "Wow, Mr. Catherman, we really sounded like a band today." That made a huge impact on me as a first-year teacher—even at the sixth-grade level the student was becoming aware of what our mission was—to reach a common goal through our musical performance, and our progress had meaning to her as a part of that group. The reward of being a music educator is simply having the opportunity/responsibility to teach—and having our students realize the results of their efforts. (Rick Catherman, instrumental music teacher, twelve years, Chelsea, MI)

Being a music educator is a powerful and meaningful career. The goal of this book is to help music educators, particularly those in the early years of their careers, to reach the point where they can experience the tremendous benefits and personal rewards of being a music educator. It is sometimes difficult for even veteran music teachers to negotiate the challenges they face on their journey towards experiencing the joy of student learning:

> I have a hard time dealing with administrators who not only do not understand your subject area, but often don't value it, and if they do, it is often in ways that are counterproductive to music education. (Instrumental music teacher, fourteen years)

I still find it hard to show up to meetings of the "co-curricular team" or the "encore team" or the "auxiliary team" or whatever they are calling us this year that reflects the "specials" nature of being a music teacher. (Elementary general music teacher, fifteen years)

In general, it's not being a creative, knowledgeable teacher that I have problems with (usually). It's trying to do all of the secretarial and administrative parts of the job. Not only do high school directors have to be teachers of music, but they have to be public relations specialists, diplomats, politicians, entertainment coordinators, fund-raising chairpersons, committee presidents, and their own secretary! That is what makes this job so hard, and that is where I struggle. If all we had to do was teach music, well, I think I would like this job a lot more than I do. (Instrumental music teacher, fourteen years)

These teachers have been fortunate in that they have managed to find support systems and mechanisms for working through the problematic issues mentioned here, and they are still teaching music. However, many new teachers entering the teaching profession are not as fortunate. Because we are currently experiencing a music teacher shortage,[1] and because research has continued to suggest that education often loses the "best and the brightest" from the field,[2] in order to draw quality teachers into the profession and retain them it is important that music teachers are properly supported and mentored. Educational research has suggested that beginning teacher induction and mentor programs are valuable and necessary for the future of education.[3]

Without proper induction into the field, new teachers will teach only as they were taught music and will not further the aims of the profession.[4] For music teachers, furthering the aims of the profession includes teaching to the National Standards for Arts Education.[5] These standards recommend many diverse content areas for music teachers (singing, playing instruments, reading music, composition, improvisation, evaluating music, connecting to other art areas, connecting to content outside the arts, providing a context for music history, etc.). High-stakes accountability programs in many states require teachers to be able to assess student learning in these areas and a variety of state variations on the standards. Many university music teacher education programs are working to prepare preservice teachers to teach within the diverse content areas outlined by the Standards. What may be missing is a mechanism for supporting beginning teachers as they leave the university and enter the music education profession.

Over the past two decades, school change experts and educational researchers have encouraged teacher educators to address induction and mentoring.[6] Only recently have music teacher educators addressed these concerns in research. Patti Krueger suggests:

The quality of music programs often depends on the continuity of their music teachers, and beginning music teachers deserve the support needed to be successful in their new profession. Positive support of ideas and programs by administrators, experienced teachers, and parents can provide the tools needed for beginning music teachers to be successful and can help new teachers stay and grow within their chosen profession.[7]

This book, *Great Beginnings for Music Teachers: Mentoring and Supporting New Teachers*, is written by music educators who have been researching the induction and mentoring of beginning music teachers. These authors have collectively worked at all levels in music education from early childhood through graduate studies and in all areas (general music, choral, and instrumental) of the profession. Each essay in the book is based on current research and provides suggestions for music mentors, music administrators, and beginning teachers. This book is timely, as many states are beginning to adopt policies for providing mentoring and induction programs to beginning teachers. Thirty-three states had such programs as of 2002.[8] I hope that the information in this book will guide state, school district, and music department decision making regarding these formal beginning teacher support systems, as well as informal music teacher mentoring and support systems.

NOTES

1. Edward Asmus, "The Increasing Demand for Music Teachers," *Journal of Music Teacher Education* 8, no. 2 (1999): 5–6; Clifford K. Madsen and Carl B. Hancock, "Support for Music Education: A Case Study of Issues Concerning Teacher Retention and Attrition," *Journal for Research in Music Education* 50, no. 1 (2002): 6–19; Music Educators National Conference, "Promoting the Profession: Recruiting and Retaining Music Teachers," *Teaching Music* 8, no. 3 (2000): 47–50.

2. National Commission on Teaching and America's Future (NCTAF), *What Matters Most: Teaching for America's Future* (Woodbridge, VA: Author, 1996); Phillip Schlechty and Victor S. Vance, "Do Academically Able Teachers Leave Education? The North Carolina Case," *Phi Delta Kappan* 63 (1981): 106–12; Phillip Schlechty and Victor S. Vance, "Recruitment, Selection, and Retention: The Shape of the Teaching Force," *Elementary School Journal* 83, no. 4 (1983): 469–87; Linda Darling-Hammond, "Keeping Good Teachers: Why It Matters, What Leaders Can Do," *Educational Leadership* 60, no. 8 (2003): 6–13; Richard Ingersoll and Thomas M. Smith, "The Wrong Solution to the Teacher Shortage," *Educational Leadership* 60, no. 8 (2003): 30–33.

3. American Federation of Teachers, "Beginning Teacher Induction: The Essential Bridge," *Educational Issues Policy Brief* no. 13 (2001); Sharon Feiman-Nemser, Sharon Schwille, Cindy Carver, and Brian Yusko, *A Conceptual Review of Literature on New Teacher Induction* (E. Lansing, MI: National Partnership of Excellence and Accountability in Teaching [NPEAT], 1999), Document #Ed449147, Sponsored by the Office of Educational Research and Improvement, Washington, DC; Yvonne Gold, "Beginning Teacher Support: Attrition, Mentoring and Induction," in *Handbook of Research on Teacher Education,* ed. J. Sikula, 2nd

ed. (New York: Macmillan, 1996), 548–94; Gary A. Griffin, ed., *The Education of Teachers. Ninety-Eighth Yearbook of the National Society for the Study of Education* (Chicago: University of Chicago Press, 1999); Leslie Huling-Austin, *Becoming a Teacher: What Research Tells Us* (Indianapolis, IN: Kappa Delta Pi Publications, 1994); Marge Scherer, ed., *A Better Beginning: Supporting and Mentoring New Teachers* (Alexandria, VA: Association for Supervision and Curriculum Development, 1999); Sharon Feiman-Nemser, "What New Teachers Need to Learn," *Educational Leadership* 60, no. 8 (2003): 25–29; National Commission on Teaching and America's Future (NCTAF), *No Dream Denied: A Pledge to America's Children* (New York: Author, 2003).

4. Sharon Feiman-Nemser, "Learning to Teach," in *Handbook of Teaching and Policy,* ed. L. Shulman and G. Sykes (New York: Longman, 1983), 150–70; Daniel Lortie, *School Teacher: A Sociological Study* (Chicago: University of Chicago Press, 1975); Sheila W. Moran, "Schools and the Beginning Teacher," *Phi Delta Kappan* 72, no. 3 (1990): 210–13; Judy Reinhartz, ed., *Teacher Induction* (Reston, VA: National Education Association, 1989); Feiman-Nemser, "What New Teachers Need to Learn."

5. Consortium of National Arts Education Associations, *National Standards for Arts Education* (Reston, VA: MENC, 1994).

6. Michael Fullan, *The New Meaning of Educational Change,* 2nd ed. (New York: Teachers College Press,1991); Seymor B. Sarason, *Revisiting the Culture of the School and the Problem of Change* (New York: Teachers College Press, 1996); Kenneth M. Zeichner and J. M. Gore, "Teacher Socialization," in *Handbook of Research on Teacher Education,* ed. Martin Haberman and John Sikula (New York: Macmillan, 1995), 329–48; Michael Fullan, *The New Meaning of Educational Change,* 3rd ed. (New York: Teachers College Press, 2001); Darling-Hammond, "Keeping Good Teachers."

7. Patti J. Krueger, "Beginning Music Teachers: Will They Leave the Profession?" *Update: Applications of Research in Music Education* 19, no. 1 (2000): 26.

8. NCTAF, "No Dream Denied."

Colleen M. Conway is assistant professor of music education at the University of Michigan School of Music.

About This Book

Great Beginnings for Music Teachers: Mentoring and Supporting New Teachers provides strategies for assisting the beginning music teacher in the challenging early years of teaching music. It describes how the music education profession is currently providing for new music teachers and suggests areas for members of the profession to consider in the future. The five sections of the book reflect research trends in the profession and include the needs of beginning music teachers (Part I), induction (Part II), mentoring (Part III), critical issues (Part IV), and listening to music teachers (Part V).

In Part I, "New Music Teacher Needs," authors provide a backdrop for the need to support beginning teachers through the difficult early years. The first essay provides an overview of research on the needs of beginning music teachers, and the second features an in-depth discussion of the specific challenges faced by teachers and provides suggestions for beginning teachers, mentors, and administrators.

Part II, "Induction," opens with a discussion of the question, "What do we as a profession really mean by induction?" The essay examines the term "induction" and questions some of the basic assumptions of beginning teacher support. The second essay in Part II provides descriptions of typical experiences of music teachers in school district-sponsored beginning teacher induction programs. In the third essay, the authors draw the reader into several specific mentoring and induction contexts. The final two essays of Part II provide concrete suggestions for how the music education profession might help address the needs of beginning music teachers in formal and informal beginning music teacher induction support initiatives.

Part III, "Mentoring," begins with a description of experiences of beginning music teachers in school district-sponsored mentoring programs. The second essay describes the Yamaha Project 2000, a successful privately funded music mentor program. "Breaking the Isolation: Beginning Music Teacher Views and Mentoring" addresses mentoring from the point of view of the beginning teacher. This chapter includes suggestions for both mentors and beginning music teachers. The final essay, "Making Mentoring Work," focuses on the pairing of mentors and mentees and offers suggestions for being a mentor.

The "Critical Issues" addressed in Part IV include the relationship between beginning teacher assistance and assessment, the often dual purposes of induction and mentoring, and the relationship between alternative certification and beginning music teacher support. "Ongoing Professional Development for Music Teachers" provides suggestions for teachers, music coordinators, staff developers, music organizations, and administrators for providing relevant professional development to music teachers throughout their careers.

Part V provides the voice of the new teacher with stories written by beginning music teachers about their experiences in the first years of teaching. These five essays explore many of the topics discussed in the research literature, including communicating the value of music education to colleagues or administration, motivating students, being left out of decision making, inadequate materials, isolation, curriculum concerns, developing rules and routines that facilitate effective classroom management, student discipline, physical exhaustion, and poor equipment/facilities.

Great Beginnings for Music Teachers: Mentoring and Supporting New Teachers is based on research with music teachers in school music programs throughout the country. The authors are indebted to the teachers in our various studies, in addition to the undergraduate and graduate students who have helped us to draw meaning from the information gathered through our work. In particular, I wish to thank Mandi Garlock and Tavia Zerman for their work with interview tape transcriptions and Stephanie Perry for research and editorial assistance. Thank you, as well, to MENC's director of professional development, Margaret A. Wang, and to MENC editor, Lisa Renfro. Last but certainly not least, I wish to acknowledge the authors of the five stories in Part V, listed here alphabetically: Rebecca G. Biber, Erin Hansen, Stephanie Perry, Jeffrey C. Stimson, and Tavia E. H. Zerman.

—*Colleen M. Conway*

PART I:
NEW MUSIC TEACHER NEEDS

What Do We Know about Beginning Music Teachers?

Colleen M. Conway

One of the early examples of research on beginning music teacher challenges was a 1977 dissertation by George Sykes Jones titled "A Descriptive Study of Problems Encountered by First-Year Instrumental Music Teachers in Oregon."[1] Jones wrote in his introduction that his study was particularly important because "many studies have sought to examine preparational deficiencies of first-year teachers. However, no study has been undertaken in the past twenty years that has sought to specifically describe problems which instrumental teachers encounter during their first years of classroom experience."[2] Jones's categories of issues faced by beginning teachers that do not necessarily relate to their teacher preparation include:

- isolation
- loneliness
- culture shock
- in-service help
- administrative help
- community relations
- feelings of failure
- feelings of being in a "sink or swim" situation
- feeling overworked
- feeling overburdened
- feeling overtired
- being confused by or in disagreement with administrative policies and evaluations
- dealing with parents
- feeling threatened, insecure, and vulnerable

The literature review section of Jones's dissertation states that the majority of the studies done in the 1950s, 60s, and 70s on beginning music teachers focused on the preparation (or lack of preparation) of these teachers in institutions of higher education. The same can be said of the beginning music teacher research conducted throughout the 70s, 80s, and 90s.[3] Although it is important for teacher educators to continue to examine teaching practices and assumptions about music teaching and learning, I believe that even the best teacher education program cannot authentically prepare a beginning teacher for the reality of the first year of teaching. Only a few studies in music education have looked beyond teacher perceptions of their preservice preparation and described challenges faced by the beginning music teacher.

Lisa DeLorenzo's survey study[4] included developing a fifty-five-item questionnaire to gather information regarding the perceived problems of beginning music teachers. She had responses from 221 beginning teachers in Pennsylvania and New Jersey. Challenging areas for music teachers highlighted in her results include (from most challenging):

- finding time to continue personal musical growth
- preparing a budget for the music program
- adapting lesson material for children with special needs
- maintaining a classroom environment with few student disruptions
- developing rules and routines that facilitate effective classroom management
- finding materials and resources for lessons
- planning sequenced learning strategies without the assistance of music textbooks or method books
- communicating the value of music education to colleagues or administration
- motivating students

Patti Krueger conducted an interactive interview study[5] with first-year teachers in Washington for the purpose of documenting teachers' perceptions of problems faced in the first year. Problems identified in this study (in order from most frequently cited problem) include:

- student discipline
- physical exhaustion
- isolation
- not teaching in primary area of expertise
- scheduling
- poor equipment/facilities
- budget concerns
- being left out of decision making

- inadequate materials
- curriculum concerns

I published a study with Mandi Garlock in 2002[6] that describes the problems Mandi faced in her first year as a K–3 general music teacher in an urban district. I think themes from this study are best represented by some of Mandi's own words:

- I was not prepared to deal with a student death, an abduction, reporting abuse, a first grader with clinical depression, and so many who had taken on anger as their coping mechanism.
- Once I had my own classroom, there was no blending into the back of the class when I wasn't feeling well, skipping if I was too tired to get up, or even relaxing when I didn't feel like being "on."
- Nobody warned me that student discipline problems are often a direct result of the barometric pressure, a windy day, the first snowfall, or especially a loss of power in an electrical storm.
- If music class is fun, why is everybody crying? It was my daily goal to make it through without someone crying, and a weekly goal to have no one bleed (not to mention wet pants, vomit, or endless trips to the bathroom).
- Throughout the year I was regularly expected to surrender my classroom and travel room to room for the sake of classroom programs, program rehearsals, assemblies, and for the PTO to make popcorn.[7]

In the next essay in this section, Paul Haack expands on this research in music and discusses its implications for beginning teachers, mentors, and administrators.

RESEARCH ON BEGINNING TEACHERS IN GENERAL EDUCATION

The literature on beginning teachers in general education includes a variety of interrelated categories: documentation of problems faced by beginning teachers, descriptions or evaluations of beginning teacher induction programs, mentoring programs for beginning teachers, stages of reflective development in new teachers, and others. I will discuss results from a sample of selected journal articles addressing problems faced by beginning teachers that I believe may be relevant to music teachers. However, issues associated with induction and mentoring programs, the development of reflection, and other issues overlap with the research issues presented here.

PROBLEMS FACED BY BEGINNING TEACHERS

Problems faced by new teachers documented in the research literature[8] that seem most relevant to music include:

- having multiple teaching assignments and difficult schedules
- being given a teaching assignment outside of their content area
- having an unrealistic vision of success
- feeling isolated
- experiencing difficulty with administrator evaluation and observation
- facing classroom management challenges
- not having enough time for planning

As I reflect on these themes in the beginning teacher literature, I would add the following about my experiences with music teachers: I have found that in many states music is a K–12 certification area,[9] music teachers are under considerable pressure to perform at a high level in public, many administrators are not familiar with the content they are observing in a music class, students in music classes are often holding "noisemakers," and the administrative responsibilities of music teachers are often enormous. It seems that the issues that are problematic for beginning teachers have the potential to be even more problematic for beginning music teachers.

CASE STUDIES OF BEGINNING TEACHERS

One of the most common formats for representing the problems of beginning teachers in the educational literature is by presenting cases of beginning teachers. Some of these cases are presented as ethnographic research cases,[10] while others are specifically formatted as teaching cases for use with preservice teachers, in-service induction and mentoring programs, and graduate students.[11] All case formats aim to describe the problems of beginning teachers through the lens of the beginning teacher. I have suggested elsewhere[12] that it may be useful for the music education community to consider building a case literature. I now suggest that some of these cases represent the voices of beginning music teachers.

Section V of this book presents cases of five beginning music teachers. Many of the beginning teacher issues discussed in these cases are supported in the research literature discussed in this chapter. The first story, "'Oh, Didn't They Tell You?'" includes references to the following: communicating the value of music education to colleagues or administration and motivating students,[13] being left out of decision making, inadequate materials, isolation, and curriculum concerns.[14] "Glad to Have My Mentor" includes discussion of "curriculum concerns"[15] and provides support for mentor research suggesting the need for a music mentor (see Part III of this book). "Searching for Diversity" includes Krueger's topic of isolation.[16] "Band Festival: A Competition or a Checkup?" includes communicating the value of music education to colleagues and administration[17] and curriculum concerns.[18] The final story, "No Teacher Left Behind,"

includes communicating the value of music education to colleagues or administration, developing rules and routines that facilitate effective classroom management, and motivating students,[19] as well as student discipline, physical exhaustion, isolation, poor equipment/facilities, and curriculum concerns.[20]

NOTES

1. George S. Jones, "A Descriptive Study of Problems Encountered by First-Year
Instrumental Teachers in Oregon" (Ph.D. diss., University of Oregon, 1977), abstract in
Dissertation Abstracts International 39 (1978): 94a.

2. Ibid., 6.

3. Richard J. Colwell, "Program Evaluation in Music Teacher Education," *Bulletin of the
Council for Research in Music Education,* no. 81 (1985): 18–64; Colleen M. Conway,
"Perceptions of Beginning Teachers, Mentors, and Administrators Regarding Preservice
Music Teacher Preparation," *Journal of Research in Music Education* 50, no. 1 (2002):
20–36; Mary A. Leglar, "A Profile of Research in Music Teacher Education," *Quarterly
Journal of Music Teaching and Learning* IV, no. 1 (1993): 59–67.

4. Lisa DeLorenzo, "Perceived Problems of Beginning Music Teachers," *Bulletin of the
Council for Research in Music Education,* no. 113 (1992): 9–25.

5. Patti J. Krueger, "Becoming a Music Teacher: Challenges of the First Year," *Dialogue
in Instrumental Music* 20, no. 2 (1996): 88–104.

6. Colleen M. Conway and Mandi Garlock, "The First Year of Teaching K–3 General
Music: A Case Study of Mandi," *Contributions to Music Education* 29, no. 2 (2002): 9–28.

7. Ibid., 17–22.

8. Sharon Feiman-Nemser, Sharon Schwille, Cindy Carver, and Brian Yusko, *A
Conceptual Review of Literature on New Teacher Induction* (E. Lansing, MI: National
Partnership of Excellence and Accountability in Teaching [NPEAT], 1999), Document
#Ed449147, Sponsored by the Office of Educational Research and Improvement,
Washington, DC; Sharon Feiman-Nemser, "What New Teachers Need to Learn," *Educational
Leadership* 60, no. 8 (2003): 25–29; Gary A. Griffin, ed., *The Education of Teachers. Ninety-
Eighth Yearbook of the National Society for the Study of Education* (Chicago: University of
Chicago Press, 1999); Daniel Lortie, *School Teacher: A Sociological Study* (Chicago:
University of Chicago Press, 1975); Marge Scherer, ed., *A Better Beginning: Supporting and
Mentoring New Teachers* (Alexandria, VA: Association for Supervision and Curriculum
Development, 1999); Linda Valli, "Beginning Teacher Problems: Areas for Teacher Education
Improvement," *Action in Teacher Education* 14, no. 1 (1992): 18–25; Susan Veenman,
"Perceived Problems of Beginning Teachers," *Review of Educational Research* 54, no. 2
(1984): 143–78.

9. According to an informal May 2003 survey of state departments of education by MENC
Information Resources, thirty states, plus the District of Columbia, offer K–12 certification for
music teachers; ten schools, as well as the Department of Defense schools, offer PreK–12
certification; and four states offer split licensure (elementary/middle/secondary). Seven states
did not respond to the survey. Sixteen of the responding states indicated that they are
currently undergoing changes in their certification programs.

10. Robert V. Bullough, *First Year Teacher: A Case Study* (New York: Teachers College
Press, 1989); Robert V. Bullough, *"First Year Teacher" Eight Years Later: An Inquiry into
Teacher Development* (New York: Teachers College Press, 1997); Jeff Kuzmic, "A Beginning

Teacher's Search for Meaning: Teacher Socialization, Organizational Literacy, and Empowerment," *Teaching and Teacher Education,* no. 10 (1994): 15–27.

11. Bullough, *First Year Teacher* and *"First Year Teacher" Eight Years Later,* Carol P. Etheridge, "Independent Action: Case Studies of its Role in Beginning Teachers' Induction," in *Teacher Induction* (Washington, DC: National Education Association, 1989), 61–73; T. J. Kowalski, R. A. Weaver, and K. T. Henson, *Case Studies of Beginning Teachers* (Boston: Addison-Wesley Publishers, 1994).

12. Colleen M. Conway, "The Case Method and Music Teacher Education," *Update: Applications of Research in Music Education* 17, no. 2 (1999): 20–26; Colleen M. Conway, "The Development of Teaching Cases for Instrumental Music Methods Courses," *Journal of Research in Music Education* 47, no. 4 (1999): 343–356.

13. DeLorenzo, "Perceived Problems of Beginning Music Teachers."

14. Krueger, "Becoming a Music Teacher."

15. Ibid.

16. Ibid.

17. DeLorenzo, "Perceived Problems of Beginning Music Teachers."

18. Krueger, "Becoming a Music Teacher."

19. DeLorenzo, "Perceived Problems of Beginning Music Teachers."

20. Krueger, "Becoming a Music Teacher."

Colleen M. Conway is assistant professor of music education at the University of Michigan School of Music.

Challenges Faced by Beginning Music Teachers

Paul Haack

Welcome to the profession! How do you feel about being legally licensed and certified as *minimally competent to teach and likely to do no serious harm!?* Well, like it or not, that is, in fact, about all the assurance that our licensure as music teachers provides. And if we're honest about it, those of us who have taught for even a little while know that regardless of how good we were as beginners, how much more competent than *minimally* we were—or thought we were—we had lots to learn.

How often have young teachers said, "I've learned as much in my first couple of years of teaching as I have in all my college years"? We felt the same way as new teachers. In fact, those who don't keep learning, and learning a lot, on the job are probably no longer in the profession. Even with the best K–12 preparation and college education, music teachers must keep right on learning and developing as music educators and as human beings. There is simply no way that new teachers can learn all there is to know before going to work in the schools. In fact, teachers at all stages of their careers must have good mentoring programs and activities, but this is particularly important for new music teachers, because their jobs are probably the most challenging of all.

So, should this situation discourage or threaten a new teacher? The answer is "No." As composer/educator Libby Larsen once said to a gathering of music teachers, "Anything worth doing is worth doing poorly at first."[1] To which could be added, "But not for long." Certainly there will be some things done poorly or even badly in the first years on the job, but good preparation will minimize flaws, and good professional development planning and mentoring will increase the odds for success.

THE MUSIC EDUCATOR'S WORK

Why is professional development so necessary—even urgent? It's necessary because new music teachers may well have the most challenging job in the teaching profession. The training that music educators receive is no more lengthy or extensive than that of other teachers, yet too often they are certified to teach K–12 instrumental, choral, and general music, in short, virtually every aspect of in-school music. So with a broad yet limited course of preparation, music educators are awarded full licensure. To make responsibilities even wider ranging, adminis-trative details come with the job, even for the beginner: equipment maintenance and repair and inventories of instruments, music, robes, and uniforms that may run into hundreds or thousands of dollars. In addition to internal school relations, public relations expectations come with the job, and thus one's work is open to general evaluation at PTA meetings, concerts, athletic meets, and community events—assessment circumstances far broader than a visit from the assistant principal every other month. These kinds of challenges and pressures can make the current teacher dropout rate even higher in the realm of music education.

There are also logistical and locational differences and difficulties. For exam-ple, it is not unusual for a new music teacher to be the only such teacher in the school, with only rare opportunity to come in contact with a music educator colleague. The music teacher is also the one with unusual classroom setups: having thirty elementary school youngsters spread all over the music room floor with their Orff instruments while he or she endeavors to help them develop creativity within the pentatonic scale framework is quite different from the inher-ently more controlled setting of youngsters doing seat work in well-ordered rows of desks. Similarly, teaching four hundred children from sixteen different class-rooms two times each per week is quite different from working with the same twenty-five children daily for most of their school time. At the middle or high school level, music educators have the added challenge of teaching an instru-mental music class of several dozen students, each and every one armed with a potent noisemaker. No other area of teaching presents novice teachers with such challenges, just as no other career usually presents its aspirants with the challenges of working at two or three different levels, under two or three differ-ent principals, in differing school and classroom settings, with two or three different faculties and staffs.

Teaching music is a unique job in many ways, so special efforts must be made to ensure that fine, energetic, and idealistic young people remain in the profession, growing well beyond the basic competence level. The loss of any potentially fine new teacher is a sad waste of time, effort, and money for the individual and for society. Developmental mentoring experiences and programs are essential to help new music educators grow and mature in a short time—and remain to teach for a long time.[2]

GENERAL EDUCATION CHALLENGES

Given all of the challenges that music teachers face, one thing needs always to be kept in mind: Teaching is the most noble of professions, and within the realm of teaching, music may well be the most noble of all.

Challenges abound in any teaching environment, in every subject matter, and at all levels of schooling. These challenges can reach a critical depth or a critical mass and become professionally life threatening, or they can be effectively anticipated and turned into growth experiences. It has been argued that, particularly for beginners, music teaching may be the most challenging of all educational endeavors. To place such a claim in context, it will be helpful to look at several basic difficulties relating to the teaching profession at large, then examine them specifically in relation to music education.

Classroom management, a euphemistic term often more appropriately abbreviated to "discipline," can be, and often is, the bane of the beginning teacher. This may be particularly true in an era of expanding class sizes. Evaluative visits and observations from the assistant principal often focus on this factor almost exclusively. Generally, it seems to be much easier to recognize a disruptive classroom environment than whether or not a teacher is employing the most appropriate method for helping a special needs child with the development of a science concept. A firm and fair manner, immediate conveyance of classroom expectations—both in terms of behavioral and educational goals—along with knowing your students both academically and personally, may be the best antidotes to disruptive, flawed learning environments. Certainly the music education challenges mentioned earlier warrant close attention in these areas.

The teaching profession lacks a well-defined career ladder for advancement. Such movement generally is limited and in the direction of administration, counseling, technology consulting, or steps on a salary schedule, if this last could be construed as career growth. Gaining acknowledgment of your expertise through mentoring or curriculum-development work may ease this situation at times, but the fact remains that the current structure of K–12 schooling does not serve the normal desire for professional advancement well. Such satisfaction may need to be gained from the more subtle accomplishments of becoming a truly fine teacher, from extracurricular work in the school, or through community service involvements in politics or other civic enterprises. The public and visible nature of many music teaching positions makes these, along with school administration, likely avenues for personal growth and/or professional advancement. Summer schedules may also allow for expanding professional growth activities in other fields such as business and industry.

Closely related to the lack of a career ladder is *the feeling of being overworked and undervalued*. As altruism fades in the face of daily reality, salary comparisons with those in professions requiring similar preparation (and similar

11

student loans) can become discouraging. It quickly becomes apparent that teaching is a high-responsibility, low-compensation occupation, and if a teacher has not recognized this from the beginning, it can readily become a challenge to remaining in the profession.

Music teachers' schedules can become burdensome, particularly with an activities-oriented curriculum. When sizable proportions of that curriculum are scheduled outside the usual school hours (and rationalized with a term such as "co-curricular"), the conventional teaching load is rarely lessened. Beginning teachers may find it difficult to request additional personnel, but established teachers in the school or district may help the newer teachers argue the case for the assistance of a paraprofessional. Also, in many districts the cooperative action of music teachers has brought about limits on the number of appearances a performing group will make at sports events, limits that not only help the teacher but also the music students maintain a more healthy and realistic pace of activities.

Teachers should be given teaching awards whenever they deserve them, and administrators should give positive reinforcement well beyond a favorable rating by the assistant principal on a routine class observation. Such recognitions may help alleviate some of the discouraging negative effects of overly critical public and political assessments of teachers and education in general whenever economic lapses bring about the need for an easy target of blame. Of course, such awards do relatively little to help teachers afford a middle-class lifestyle.

Related misunderstandings about "having summers off" and thus not deserving a wage commensurate with four or five years of college preparation is another challenge to maintaining a positive attitude about teaching. Unfortunately, teachers still have living expenses during the "summer off," and frequently these are greater than during the school year, because teachers are expected to spend thousands of dollars of sparse income on additional schooling and work toward a graduate degree. (If such self-improvement expenses instead were invested, the monetary return would likely be much greater than any potential gains on a teaching salary schedule.)

Salary schedules themselves can be a challenge to beginning teachers because they are not the normal approach to pay in occupations that require college degrees and are considered professional. These occupations generally offer merit- and effort-based pay and are more under the control of the individual. The beginning teacher, however, is locked into the low end of a salary schedule regardless of accomplishment for a period long enough that he or she may consider other career alternatives.

When the drain on a relatively modest salary includes payments on a hefty student loan, the music teacher faces further challenges. Benefits beyond the intangible rewards of aiding in the development of young people are few.

However, teacher educators can help aspiring music teachers by recognizing and openly discussing such challenges to satisfaction, success, and longevity in the teaching profession during the college preparation years.

An additional challenge to the beginning teacher in any curricular area is a condition commonly called *burnout*. Usually this factor is not regarded as a threat until a teacher has taught for five to ten years. However, the roots of burnout may well be grounded in the establishment of habits and routines that date back to the beginnings of the teaching experience. All of the other challenges faced by teachers can contribute to burnout, and beginning teacher mentoring programs need to take this into account.

General burnout concerns may include heavy teaching loads, great time commitments, large classes, fatigue, lack of variety, boredom, paperwork related to social and health issues rather than subject matter issues, and unclear goals and standards in terms of student achievement.[3] In my own casual observations made over decades, I have noticed that class sizes and teaching loads seem to vary more with economic conditions than with research-based estimates of student achievement. Political involvement may be the most effective, if not the only, way to deal with such realities.

The large time commitments required of any good teacher in any subject matter area are even more demanding for newer teachers who are contending with much on-the-job learning. Again, good mentoring will help, but in reality, reduced loads for first- and second-year teachers could be a good investment in the long run, particularly in terms of retention. Job-oriented fatigue, stress, and anxiety generally affect the beginning teacher more than the veteran, but added factors such as lack of variety and boredom can make the possibilities of burnout almost as threatening for experienced teachers. The development of solid peer and mentor relationships can help here, as can more personal matters such as diet, exercise, sports, and further educational endeavors.[4]

Issues not directly related to a teacher's teaching area, such as much paperwork, forms, and reporting, can seem like inefficient use of a professional's time, particularly when the profession is under fire for what some consider a lack of educational results. However, if teachers can see the links between these social concerns and learning achievements, even beginning teachers may be more motivated to deal with such matters. Preservice education courses, on-the-job in-service experiences, and administrative leadership can help teachers understand the need for such work—and minimize it.

Finally, we are in a time of confusion about educational goals and standards, but this is not a new situation. The basic issue appears to be a part of the ongoing debates about broadly oriented general education as a value in and of itself versus educational curricula for more specific utilitarian purposes; education as a personal, social, and civic good versus education to develop more effective

13

employees and a stronger economy. The goals situation becomes even less clear when these competing interests are being manifested in varying ways at different levels of government. And the confusion becomes even more challenging when varying testing philosophies enter the arena. Possibly the best response a newer professional can make is to study the issues in the cooler contexts of history and philosophy and develop a sensible rationale for one's own beliefs, while recognizing and respecting the vacillations that are a part of life and education in a relatively free, capitalistic society.

While the foregoing list of concerns is by no means exhaustive, it does exemplify the breadth of issues that confront beginning teachers in any subject area. Some of these matters will be revisited as the focus of discussion turns to the more specific aspects of challenges that face beginning *music* teachers.

MUSIC EDUCATION CHALLENGES

The previous chapter, "What Do We Know about Beginning Music Teachers?" includes brief outlines and general findings of several studies that deal with such challenges. Now, two of these studies will be examined in some depth for their points of agreement and differences and for their helpfulness in understanding the challenges faced by beginning music teachers.

DeLorenzo[5] and Krueger[6] used mail survey and personal interview techniques, respectively, to solicit and rank lists of concerns from their beginning teacher subjects. As mentioned in "What Do We Know about Beginning Music Teachers?" DeLorenzo identified nine major areas of concern, and Krueger listed ten. The fact that areas of concern were not always discrete and the issue of semantics made direct comparisons difficult at times. Nevertheless, many interesting and worthwhile observations may be gleaned from this work.

Student discipline heads Krueger's list. Related items on DeLorenzo's list are ranked four and five: *disruption-free environment* and *rules and routines for effective classroom management.* Possibly even more so in music than other subjects, administrators responsible for the evaluation of new teachers tend to focus on orderliness in the class or rehearsal room. This may be because music teaching methods seem more unique and specialized (thus the term "music specialist"?) than those employed in most other curricular areas. The variety and intricacies of music itself may be more of a mystery for some administrators. For whatever reason (and based on my own casual observation), the great preponderance of the commentary resulting from the evaluative visits relates to classroom or rehearsal room management.

Because of the extraordinary challenges that music teachers face— challenges such as an activities-based curriculum, performing ensembles two or three times the normal class size, and every student being equipped with a tempting noisemaker—it is essential that rules and routines that facilitate the communication necessary to effective learning be established from "day one." This, however, needs to be a concern long before the first day of teaching. Effective leadership techniques can be developed in a high school teacher's or director's assistant role as soon as a vocational interest in music teaching is identified. Then these matters must continue to be discussed early and often, such as in the college "Introduction to Music Education" class and in related observations in the schools. Student teaching must provide special opportunities and guidance as responsibilities gradually shift to the student teacher.

Along with effective rules and routines gleaned from much observation, the best preventative practice is to be well prepared for the class or rehearsal so that the learning activities keep moving without undue pause or delay. Of course unanticipated events occur, and there is no substitute for a wealth of experience in turning unexpected deviations from the lesson plan into positive experiences. The point is that this kind of experience needs to be accumulating from the day that a young musician realizes he or she wants to become a music teacher. This may be as early as middle school, and there is no substitute for early mentoring and leadership experience.[7]

Because *motivation* is closely related to classroom management, it is considered at this point even though it was ranked ninth on DeLorenzo's list and not mentioned as such on Krueger's list. It is important for enthusiastic new music educators to realize and keep in mind that most of their student musicians enjoy music but simply are not as devoted to it as they themselves are. This is particularly true when we think in terms of the normal content of *school* music. Nevertheless, the teacher's apparent enthusiasm for the subject, reasonably high standards, the careful selection of a good sampling of various musics to vitalize the curriculum, along with comprehensive general music goals including the realization of music's uses, functions, and values, will not only provide motivation but will also go a long way toward the solution to class management challenges.

Budget concerns appeared in both listings, second on DeLorenzo's and seventh on Krueger's. Challenges in this area ranged from the basics of how to formulate a budget document to how to advocate for the necessary resources. While some principals simply provide a monetary limit for program expenditures, a more formal budget document and process can be a valuable learning interaction between music teacher and administrator. The costs of music, new instruments, instrument maintenance, and program-related travel can add up to much more than either realize, and getting it on the table, in writing, can be helpful. If music is to be recognized as a legitimate educational activity, supplementing curricular aspects of the music program with student fund-raising activities needs to be avoided.

Curriculum-related concerns could also be construed to appear on both lists, tenth on Krueger's and seventh (sequencing learning activities without textbooks) as well as third (adapting material for special needs children) on DeLorenzo's. Related also is the matter of *materials*, a concern that was ranked sixth on DeLorenzo's list and ninth on Krueger's. Fortunately, the curriculum reform and standards movements of the latter twentieth century, along with the movement initially termed "mainstreaming" for special needs children, have had notable effects on elementary-level music education, including the development of many texts and related materials.

Similar effects have not been as notable at the secondary level and particularly not in the more exclusive "music education through performance" venues. In higher-level performance, technical goals and necessities tend to compete for time and attention with conceptual developments, with the latter frequently receiving less attention. Nevertheless, there is some isolated but excellent work going on in some schools, and at the state level, the efforts of the Wisconsin Music Educators Association in developing a truly "comprehensive music" curriculum need to be recognized. At the national level, the American Composers Forum's "BandQuest" project is notable for its development of school-oriented compositions and related teaching and learning materials. Such models and materials need to be a part of methods classes and should be sought out by beginning music teachers wherever they can be found.

Music was one of the first subject areas to involve *special needs children,* even before the term "mainstreaming" was coined. This generally was limited to the elementary level, for which a considerable amount of material has now been developed. Still, music teachers working with special needs children at any level should be in close contact with the special education faculty (as well as with music therapists, if available in the district) and should exercise their creativity, musical as well as methodological, to develop music parts and materials that can accommodate all students in a given setting. Also, teacher aids should be requested and used when children (and teachers) need special help in an ensemble or classroom setting.

Two closely related matters are *advocacy* for the importance of music education, particularly among colleagues and administrators (eighth on DeLorenzo's list), and concern about being *left out of decision making* (eighth on Krueger's list). Many materials are now available to assist the beginning teacher in advocacy efforts, and one of the real challenges is to avoid making specious claims and coming to dubious conclusions based on the available research. Colleagues, administrators, and school board members are, or should be, aware of the difference between correlation and causation, an often misconstrued situation. Music education may truly be among the most potent, valuable, and far-reaching aspects of the curriculum, but it still is important to interpret research findings validly in attempting to support it and not try to make music look like a snake oil elixir for all the ills of education.

Of course, appropriate advocacy efforts can be an effective antidote to being left out of the decision-making process. Music educators often have large workloads with related activities before and after school. Nevertheless, if they are too busy for faculty meetings and committee service, they *will* be left out of the decision-making process, and some of the decisions will surely affect them, their programs, and their students. The major longstanding challenge for all music educators, not just beginners, is to be a part of the school, to be a colleague and a consultant to faculty who want to use music in teaching their own subject matter, and to be a part of the total educational environment so as to be a more effective music educator. This can be a particular challenge for a teacher working at two or three sites, but even in such situations, a teacher can work with administrators to establish a home base and have time to participate more fully in the processes of that school.

Scheduling, closely related to the issues of being involved in decision making and being a part of the entire educational environment, appeared fifth in Krueger's rankings. Decisions such as moving to a four-period day do not come out of the blue. Music educators must be sure that they offer input related to the best possible teaching environment for music education, but they also need to develop a broader understanding of the curriculum at large. They need to become aware of how others are facing such challenges, and they need the creativity to devise and suggest options and adaptations and make the best of what may at first appear to be a devastating problem. Again, being a recognizable part of the school and the curriculum can go a long way toward gaining compromises and developing arrangements that favor K–12 music education in the long run.

Another aspect of scheduling can be a pitfall for newer music educators, especially those involved with the secondary school curriculum. This has to do with the time and other needs of students in performance programs. Extracurricular and out-of-school time expectations such as concerts, trips, and athletic services need to be the result of reasonable determinations made by music teachers, administrators, and athletic directors working together. Such expectations need to be clear and well-known to all concerned early on, or they will inevitably detract from the essential curricular side of the music program.

Of those challenges appearing on only one list, *time for personal musical growth* ranked number one in DeLorenzo's study. The reasons many choose the music education profession include a love for music and music making and the desire to share that love. Personal creative urges can seldom be totally satisfied in the classroom or even the high school rehearsal room. This need was recognized most notably and clearly in the MENC publication *Music Teacher Education: Partnership and Process* [8] where not only professional growth concerns but also *personal* growth concerns were listed and discussed extensively. (See Chapter 3, "Professional Development Programs: Planning for Career Growth," by Paul Haack and Jeffrey Kimpton, excerpted later in this book on pages 157–63.)

Haack and Kimpton's chapter notes that the well-planned, orderly "process for continued growth and professional advancement is linked to the support provided by an ever-expanding partnership of advisers."[9] This theme will be expanded upon in subsequent chapters of this book but is relevant to meeting every one of the concerns addressed in this current chapter. Of particular interest for the challenges under consideration is the recognition of the need for "individualized professional development, to provide specific opportunities for personal growth."[10] This forward-looking document listed four types of growth challenges under the heading "Individualized Professional Development": personal, intellectual, musical, and instructional.[11] DeLorenzo's listing specified the challenge of finding time particularly for personal musical growth, and *Partnership and Process* provided several examples of these kinds of musical growth activities that can be chosen and for which time must be reserved: performance in one's major area or a secondary medium; development of improvisation skills or composition skills; development of expertise in music theory, history, or ethnomusicology; development of professional leadership skills in philosophical or sociological areas; and so forth.[12]

The ability to prioritize is an important skill for newer professionals trying to find time for musical (and other) growth and in dealing with another challenge: physical exhaustion. Mentoring assistance can be particularly helpful here. The above-cited examples of directions for personal musical growth are a vital base for good teaching and give professionals a source of credibility in their roles as music educators and community music leaders.

Physical exhaustion was ranked second on Krueger's list, and this is understandable considering the long hours and physical nature of music teaching at any level. While most accept these conditions as a fact of the music educator's life, it is important to go beyond mere recognition to *prevention* of likely consequences. An effective but busy routine must include rest and good dietary habits. Personal musical and other activities such as reading and exercising can help ward off exhaustion, but the foremost concern must be to place limits on the amount of time on the job. Again, the professional credibility earned by good music teaching and related abilities should make administrators open to the need for a reasonable schedule and additional help when necessary. Good advocacy skills and kind persistence are valuable allies.

Isolation, third on Krueger's list, is often brought on at least in part by music teachers themselves. "There just isn't time to interact meaningfully with other teachers" may be the excuse, but the educational system must share the blame. The Yamaha Project 2000 included a mentoring program sponsored jointly by the Yamaha Corporation of America, the University of Minnesota School of Music, and the Minnesota Music Educators Association. Early in the program, a first-year teacher appeared at a monthly dinner meeting with tears in her eyes. She explained in response to the concern of her colleagues that they were tears of joy. She had not come in contact with another music teacher since the previous meeting, and she was happy to be able to interact with colleagues again, even if only for a little while.

This young woman taught at three elementary schools. There was no music supervisor at the time, and she was on her own in a large district. Furthermore, the school system allowed teachers to move, on a seniority basis, to other school positions that opened up each year. This had the result of putting her and many other new teachers in the least desirable and most difficult environments!

In performance music classes, isolation is often exacerbated by architectural designs that locate the "noisy" subjects at the far end of the building. The temptation for super-busy teachers to isolate themselves in their own little "fiefdoms" is thus aided and abetted. These kinds of challenges make it all the more necessary for new teachers to have mentors to help counteract the isolation and to find ways to interact with and become friends with teachers from other areas of the curriculum.

Not teaching in primary areas of expertise is ranked fourth on Krueger's list and may well be a growing concern. In recent years there has been pressure from legislators for more liberal licensure, including certifications that authorize music educators to teach at all levels and in all areas of music education, a situation that can be particularly challenging for beginning music teachers. However, as long as governors and legislatures, and indirectly the public, support policies that in effect say, "we don't want to give schools more money, but as a trade off, we'll give administrators more flexibility in staffing," the quality of education will be threatened.

It is easy to tell someone who is assigned classes outside of his or her comfort zone to take some more course work to become competent. This is generally less threatening for veteran teachers than for beginners who are still trying to get their acts together. Clearly, however, it would be wise for newer teachers who can at least temporarily avoid or survive such circumstances to spend some of their expected continuing education or professional development studying in their certification areas of *least* comfort. A teacher could then become more useful to his or her district and students and more likely to be retained if and when serious staffing difficulties arise.

Sixth on Krueger's list is the challenge of having to work with *inadequate equipment and facilities*. Beginning teachers need to be well aware of budget processes. They need to be able to develop replacement-and-addition schedules for all of the program's equipment and music and discuss them with their colleagues and administrators. Safety must be a prime concern. Effective sound treatment and room tuning is vital for good rehearsal and teaching space, for students, and for the hearing health of teachers who spend most of their school time in such an environment.

When new or refurbished facilities are being considered by a district, music teachers may have the community on their side. This is particularly true of performance facilities that can be shared and will enhance the community. Community drama and music organizations can be effective allies, but try never to blindside your administrator by not going through proper channels when resources or other needs become an issue. In fact, when repair or replacement schedules are to be discussed, get copies of the proposal to your administrator well ahead of your meeting. He or she will appreciate it, and you will reach agreement more readily.

Then and Now

One additional list of challenges will be considered, a fairly detailed compilation of items intended for use primarily as a needs assessment instrument for newer teachers. It was developed in 1990 by Paul Haack and Michael Smith, project coordinators, as a tool for the "Mentoring" portion of the Yamaha Project 2000. It was used for several years at that time and has recently been used again in an effort to provide some insight into how the perceived needs of newer music teachers may have changed over the course of more than a decade.

What is reported here is at best an exploratory or pilot study, and, while it demonstrates some very interesting possibilities in terms of findings, sample sizes are small and not necessarily representative of music educators in general. The survey respondents consisted of groups of newer music teachers from two different, large metropolitan areas of the upper Midwest. Without drawing any firm conclusions, it may be useful to review the variety of challenges and note how they might have changed over time.

The very recent (April, 2003) survey data resulted from a sample of twenty-four teachers, while the earlier (1990–93) data came from samples totaling fifty-six teachers. The teachers had an average of two years of K–12 teaching experience. Table 1 lists the earlier rankings, the recent rankings, and the change in rankings for each of the twenty-five items. Subjects were asked to rate each item on a 1–10 scale, with 1 representing an area of *great* concern/*dis*comfort. In the change column, a minus (-) indicates less concern now than earlier, and a plus (+) indicates more concern now than earlier (25 items, A through Y).

TABLE 1. NEEDS OF NEW MUSIC TEACHERS

1990–93	2003	Change	Item
1	25	- 24	A. Computer skills
2.5	15.5	- 13	B. Skills with other educational/musical technology
6.5	19.5	- 13	C. Instructional design/curriculum development
9	19.5	- 10.5	D. Student evaluation and grading
15.5	24	- 8.5	E. Daily class planning and organization
8	15.5	- 7.5	F. Knowledge of teaching materials and music literature
5	12	- 7	G. Music program administration
10.5	15.5	- 5	H. Knowledge of teaching methods
4	8.5	- 4.5	I. Classroom (music room) management/discipline
15.5	18	- 2.5	J. Rationalizing (advocating/defending) music in the curriculum
18.5	21	- 2.5	K. Problem-solving skills
21	23	- 2	L. Communication skills
2.5	4	- 1.5	M. Knowledge of administrative/political structures & procedures
6.5	5.5	+ 1	N. Special learner accommodations
25	22	+ 3	O. Interpersonal skills
15.5	11	+ 4.5	P. Understanding and using research
18.5	13	+ 5.5	Q. Rehearsal skills
24	15.5	+ 8.5	R. Knowledge of music fundamentals, history, literature
15.5	7	+ 8.5	S. Applied learning theory
12	3	+ 9	T. Ethnic/multicultural music education
10.5	1	+ 9.5	U. Improvising skills
13	2	+ 11	V. Arranging/composing skills
20	8.5	+ 11.5	W. Social/psychological uses and functions of music
22.5	10	+ 12.5	X. Conducting skills
22.5	5.5	+ 17	Y. Keyboard skills

While extreme caution should be taken in interpreting or attempting to generalize from these data, there are quite a few notable items and shifts that could raise interesting questions for future research relating to challenges in the profession.

Most dramatic of the large changes from major challenges to matters of little or no concern is "Computer skills" (item A in Table 1), which shifted from the area of greatest discomfort in the early 1990s to the current item of least discomfort. In just over a decade, computer availability and education seem to have virtually done away with the challenges associated with using computers in music education.

"Skills with other educational/musical technology" (B) and "Instructional design/curriculum development" (C) are tied for second after "Computer skills" for former areas of concern that music teachers no longer find as challenging as they did previously. Relationships and reinforcements could readily be noted that help account for the changes in these areas.

Items that formerly were ranked in the moderate to low concern areas but are now regarded among the top ten challenges include "Improvising skills" (U), Arranging/composing skills" (V), and "Ethnic/multicultural music education" (T). According to the recent survey data, these are currently the top three challenges for newer music teachers. Also moving notably up the ladder of concerns is "Social/psychological uses and functions of music" (W). These changes might be, at least in part, due to and consistent with recent curricular movements related to the development of more comprehensive standards and goals for music education. The more traditional areas of "Conducting skills" (X) and "Keyboard skills" (Y) also shifted from ratings of comfort to concern.

Those areas that were formerly considered to be major challenges and remain so in the current rankings include "Classroom/music room management/discipline" (I), "Knowledge of administrative/political structures and procedures" (M), and "Special learner accommodations" (N). These rankings are consistent with findings presented earlier.

Also, "Knowledge of music fundamentals, history, literature" (R) moved from an area of great comfort to a more moderate ranking, while the reverse was noted for "Daily class planning and organization" (E). Other shifts include "Student evaluation and grading" (D), "Knowledge of teaching materials and music literature" (F), and "Music program administration" (G) moving from top-ten needs positions to more moderate rankings.

Areas that were, and still are, ranked in the moderate range include "Knowledge of teaching methods" (H), "Rationalizing/advocating/defending music in the curriculum" (J), "Understanding and using research" (P), "Rehearsal skills" (Q), and "Applied learning theory" (S).

Finally, items that were, and still are, ranked as very comfortable include "Communication skills" (L), "Interpersonal skills" (O), and "Problem-solving skills"

(K). These areas also could be considered closely related, and, given the modest amount of formal curricular attention to such matters, it is interesting to speculate on their roles relating to "self-selection" into the profession.

RETENTION AND ATTRITION

In conclusion, it may be fitting to share several observations and implications about challenges for the beginning music teacher from the most recently published research in the area of retention and attrition. Becoming productive professionals or burning out and leaving are the likely outcomes of successfully meeting or not meeting the challenges of a beginning teacher. Again, the stage is being set for these outcomes from day one.

Madsen and Hancock's study[13] provided data that reinforced the impression that many newer music teachers continue to leave the profession early in their careers. Music teacher survey respondents expressed concern about several issues, including a lack of administrative support. Apparently, administrators are frequently perceived as regarding music as more of an extracurricular than curricular or basic aspect of education. At the secondary level, music tends to be regarded solely for its service and utilitarian functions, and at the elementary level it is seen primarily as a vehicle to provide a break or prep time for "academic" teachers. Clearly, music educators must learn to educate more than just their students.

Teacher comments relating to music teaching time demands at the expense of personal and other professional needs also reinforced issues discussed earlier in this chapter. In addition, feelings of isolation echoed prior concerns. The possibilities of therapeutic as well as professional development assistance from peer interactions at local, state, and national conferences should not be overlooked, nor should beginning music teachers be excluded from these opportunities on the basis of seniority, particularly when they may have the greatest need for such experiences.

A CLOSING CHALLENGE

The prime challenge for the beginning music teacher and for anyone just beginning to think about becoming a music teacher is to understand the big picture: to know yourself and particularly your values and to know the profession with its wonderful students and satisfactions—along with its difficulties and pitfalls. Part of that challenge is being honest with yourself about being a teacher every bit as much as being a musician. Early in the decision stages you must seek the help you need to see yourself as a *music educator*, not only as a band or orchestra director or a choral conductor (even though band, orchestra, or chorus may well be what attracted you to the profession in the first place). This self-concept needs to be nurtured and allowed to grow through the years of

23

preparation and beginning teaching if success, joy, and teaching longevity are to be achieved.

Madsen and Hancock mention the need to equip beginning teachers for the changing demands that a changing society puts on today's educators. Maybe the greatest challenge of all, and the one that will fall heaviest on the shoulders of today's beginning teachers, is that the music education profession, like others, is struggling to understand and come to terms with twenty-first-century needs. Such understanding may well result in a shift away from many twentieth-century paradigms. Thus, above all, twenty-first-century beginning music teachers must prepare themselves for professional leadership, because change is the real challenge.

NOTES

1. Keynote speech, Minnesota Music Educators state conference, Minneapolis, 17 February 1994.

2. The preceding was excerpted from Paul Haack and Michael V. Smith, "Mentoring New Music Teachers," *Music Educators Journal* 87, no. 3, (2000): 23–26; reprinted with permission.

3. R. Pembrook and C. Craig, "Teaching as a Profession," in *The New Handbook of Research on Music Teaching and Learning*, ed. R. Colwell and C. Richardson (Oxford: Oxford University Press, 2002), 786–817.

4. Pembrook and Craig, "Teaching as a Profession."

5. Lisa DeLorenzo, "Perceived Problems of Beginning Music Teachers," *Bulletin of the Council for Research in Music Education,* no. 113 (1992): 9–25.

6. Patti J. Krueger, "Becoming a Music Teacher: Challenges of the First Year," *Dialogue in Instrumental Music* 20, no. 2 (1996): 88–104.

7. See Chapter One of G.B. Olson, ed., *Music Teacher Education: Partnership and Process* (Reston, VA: MENC, 1987).

8. Olson, *Music Teacher Education.*

9. Ibid., 41.

10. Ibid., 41.

11. Ibid., 45–46.

12. Ibid., 46.

13. Clifford K. Madsen and Carl B. Hancock, "Support for Music Education: A Case Study of Issues Concerning Teacher Retention and Attrition," *Journal for Research in Music Education* 50, no. 1 (2002): 6–19.

Paul Haack is professor of music education at the University of Minnesota.

PART II:

INDUCTION

What Is Induction?

Colleen M. Conway

> What happens to beginning teachers during their early years on the job determines not only whether they will stay in teaching but also what kind of teacher they become.[1]

Back in 1977, music educator George Jones discussed the concept of induction in his dissertation.[2] He framed his discussion around the work of noted educational researcher James Conant, who states:

> No such program—in my judgment, no kind of preservice program—can prepare first-year teachers to operate effectively in the "sink-or-swim" situation in which they too often find themselves. Many local school boards have, I believe, been scandalously remiss in failing to give adequate assistance to new teachers.[3]

Although made in 1963, Conant's recommendations regarding induction are still relevant for programs today. He suggests:

> During the initial probationary period, local school boards should take specific steps to provide the new teacher with every possible help in the form of: (a) limited teaching responsibility; (b) aid in gathering instructional materials; (c) advice of experienced teachers whose own load is reduced so that they can work with the new teacher in his own classroom; (d) shifting to more experienced teachers those pupils who create problems beyond the ability of the novice to handle effectively; and (e) specialized instruction concerning the characteristics of the community, the neighborhood, and the students he is likely to encounter.[4]

Several decades after the Jones report, the participants in Lisa DeLorenzo's study[5] reported that school district-sponsored induction programs were the least

27

helpful beginning music teacher support systems. DeLorenzo reported that "the perceived value of these programs (mentor and induction) were as varied as the programs themselves."[6] This lack of consistency in and high degree of dissatisfaction with induction programs has continued to be documented in beginning music teacher induction research.[7]

However, school district-sponsored induction support programs have continued to be recommended as a means to retain beginning teachers and help them succeed.[8] Researchers, practitioners, and policy makers have worked together to create models and frameworks for successful general teacher induction programs. Many of these programs have been evaluated through research.[9] Although beginning teacher induction remains an area of interest for educators,[10] these general teacher induction studies do not discuss the induction needs of music teachers. Conway, Krueger, Robinson, Haack, and Smith[11] suggest that the research that forms the basis for educational policy may not reflect the needs of the beginning music teacher population.

Three music education studies have examined music teacher induction programs specifically.[12] All three studies suggest that induction programs that provide content-specific information were perceived by music teachers as useful. However, it is rare in district-sponsored induction programs for music-specific content to be a part of the program.

Beginning music teacher induction is not merely about retaining teachers in the field. It is about fostering growth in beginning teachers so that they emerge from the induction phase as reflective master music teachers. Feiman-Nemser et al. suggest that in general education "standards-based reforms calling for more challenging teaching and learning, projections of teacher shortages and data about teacher attrition have contributed to a growing consensus that support and assistance are essential to the retention and effectiveness of beginning teachers."[13] As we consider music teachers within the population of general teachers, it would seem that the National Standards for Music Education[14] certainly call for reforming the way music is taught and learned. Most preservice programs align undergraduate music education course work with the National Standards in some way. However, if we as a profession expect novice teachers to be able to push the profession towards the standards-based model of instruction and assessment, we must provide opportunities for beginning teachers to grapple with the differences between what they experienced as students in non-standards-based programs, what they often experience as student teachers, what their preservice education suggested to them, and what they are being encouraged to embrace as beginning teachers. Designing those opportunities for music teachers is what I refer to as "induction."

Feiman-Nemser et al. outline three meanings or uses of the term "induction." The first use of the term "induction" is as a label for the stage or phase of teacher development that occurs during the first years of teaching. They suggest that researchers working within this definition of induction "tend to emphasize the self-defined problems and concerns of beginning teachers rather than the central tasks of learning to teach."[15]

The second use of the term "induction" refers to a time of transition or socialization when teachers are moving from teacher preparation to teaching practice. Studies that embrace this definition of induction often examine the beginning teachers' occupational setting and professional community in order to document the messages teachers receive about what it means to be a teacher and how these messages influence the teachers' emerging identity and practice.

Feiman-Nemser et al. suggest that the third definition of "induction" refers to a formal program for beginning teachers. This definition fits most closely with my use of the term throughout this book. Feiman-Nemser and her colleagues' statement that the level of consistency at the national level about what is considered an "induction program" varies greatly is supported by other research on beginning music teachers.[16] Feiman-Nemser et al. also state that "thinking about induction as a phase in teacher development and a process of teacher socialization reminds us that, for better or worse, induction happens with or without a formal program."[17]

When I speak to experienced teachers about my work with beginning teachers in both formal and informal induction programs, I often hear comments such as: "I guess I don't understand these kids today. No one provided an induction or mentor program for me. I went out and found somebody to ask when I needed to know something. It seems like we are babying these kids." What concerns me about this general attitude is that beginning teachers who are inducted by this approach are sent a negative message. Music teaching does not have to be a competitive, fairly isolated interaction between a teacher and a group of students. The "I always fended for myself" attitude unfortunately encourages this type of teacher isolation. Quotes from some beginning music teachers highlight this issue:

When I went to my first local music organization meeting no one really spoke to me. I mean, I was the new guy and I guess I should have run around and introduced myself, but I was sort of waiting for someone to say—hey, welcome to this part of the state. (First-year teacher)

I know this sounds bad, but as I think about my colleagues around here, no one really had anything to say to me the first two years. This district has had so many directors that I guess they just figured I was a short-timer too. Then, this year when my bands got really high ratings at festival (for the first time) all of a sudden people wanted to know who I was. I sort of felt like, where were you when I needed you? I have it figured out now. (Third-year teacher)

A Problematic Music Education Model

It has been my experience that beginning music teachers are often "inducted" into a program by being provided with "this is how it works around here" information. This comes from administrators, parents, and students just as often as it comes from other music teachers. What I have sometimes seen in formal induction programs is the same attitude. I worry that in our effort to support beginning music teachers we may be robbing them of the opportunity to make changes both inside the profession and in society at large. Although they have not been in a situation to try out their ideas in teaching practice, most music teachers graduate from preservice programs with some ideas about music teaching and learning. If their only experiences with colleagues in early induction programs center around maintaining the status quo, then the profession is losing the opportunity to continue improving music teaching and learning.

A Common Error in Music Induction Programs

When induction is narrowly defined as short-term support to help teachers survive their first year on the job, its role in fostering quality teaching and learning is diminished.[18]

Many of the music induction programs I have observed are presented to beginning teachers as survival sessions. Workshop titles I have seen include "Music Teachers Survival Camp," "What They Didn't Teach You in College About Being a Music Teacher," "Strategies for Getting Through the First Year," and "Everything You Need To Survive That First Year as a Music Teacher," among others. As Sharon Feiman-Nemser and her colleagues suggest, if induction is seen as a first-year survival program, then the kind of effect that the program can have on real teacher growth is minimal.

RESOURCES FOR CREATING BEGINNING TEACHER INDUCTION PROGRAMS

Gordon, Stephen P., and Susan Maxey. *How to Help Beginning Teachers Succeed*, 2nd ed. (Alexandria, VA: Association for Supervision and Curriculum Development, 2000).

MacDonald, Robert E., and Sean D. Healy. *A Handbook for Beginning Teachers*, 2nd ed. (New York: Longman, 1999).

Moffatt, Courtney W., and Thomas L. Moffatt. *Handbook for the Beginning Teacher* (Boston: Allyn and Bacon, 2003).

Roehrig, Alysia D., Michael Pressley, and Denise Talotta. *Stories of Beginning Teachers* (Notre Dame, IN: University of Notre Dame Press, 2002).

Scherer, Marge, ed. *A Better Beginning: Supporting and Mentoring New Teachers* (Alexandria, VA: Association for Supervision and Curriculum Development, 1999).

Wilke, Rebecca L. *The First Days of Class—A Practical Guide for the Beginning Teacher* (Thousand Oaks, CA: Corwin, 2003).

Wong, Harry K., and Rosemary T. Wong. *The First Days of School* (Mountain View, CA: Harry K. Wong Publications, 1998).

This is not to say that music teacher "survival days" (often sponsored by the music industry) should be removed from the teacher's experience. However, all of us in the profession must recognize that merely presenting short-term survival strategies is not enough. (For a list of useful induction resources, see the Resources for Creating Beginning Teacher Induction Programs sidebar.)

INDUCTION BEYOND THE FIRST YEAR

Many states recognize that the period of growth for a beginning teacher goes beyond the first year. However, I have observed that although the induction phase may be considered the period of time until tenure (three or four years), induction programs are geared primarily towards the first year. Teachers in their second, third, and fourth year are often troubled by issues that go beyond survival, as the following comments from music teachers illustrate:

> The first year I was just worried about getting through every day. Now I actually want to get through every day and be good at it. (Second-year music teacher)

> Does it seem weird to you that this job is getting harder? I feel like the longer I teach the less I know about being a teacher. (Third-year music teacher)

> So I have lots of things figured out, but I still don't think I'm so good. My list of things I need to know more about is a mile long. (Fourth-year music teacher)

All good teachers know that learning to teach is a career-long endeavor. However, many teachers leave the profession in the first five years due to frustration. If the profession can help support teachers throughout this five-year period, we may have a better chance of retaining them.

I have worked with beginning teachers who are not asking questions about improving themselves and their classrooms. Some of these teachers get through the survival stage of the first year and settle into a "teaching groove" that works for them. It is hard to watch beginning teachers teach their second year for the rest of their career. These teachers mean well, they like kids, and they try to make connections for students. However, they lack the reflective capacity to continue to grow. Recognizing the need for induction support beyond the first year will not only help to retain the reflective teachers, but it may also help make reflective teachers of those who are not naturally so. Part IV of this book provides more details and specifics for ongoing professional development support for music teachers.

NOTES

1. Sharon Feiman-Nemser, Sharon Schwille, Cindy Carver, and Brian Yusko, *A Conceptual Review of Literature on New Teacher Induction* (E. Lansing, MI: National Partnership of Excellence and Accountability in Teaching [NPEAT], 1999), 1. Document #Ed449147, Sponsored by the Office of Educational Research and Improvement, Washington, DC.

2. George S. Jones, "A Descriptive Study of Problems Encountered by First-Year Instrumental Teachers in Oregon" (Ph.D. diss., University of Oregon, 1977), abstract in *Dissertation Abstracts International* 39 (1978): 94a.

3. James B. Conant, *The Education of American Teachers* (New York: McGraw-Hill, 1963), 70. Quoted in Jones, "A Descriptive Study of Problems Encountered by First-Year Instrumental Teachers in Oregon."

4. Ibid., 70–71.

5. Lisa DeLorenzo, "Perceived Problems of Beginning Music Teachers," *Bulletin of the Council for Research in Music Education,* no. 113 (1992): 9–25.

6. Ibid., 20.

7. Colleen M. Conway, "Beginning Music Teacher Perceptions of District-sponsored Induction Programs," *Bulletin of the Council for Research in Music Education,* no. 151 (2001): 1–11; Patti J. Krueger, "New Music Teachers Speak out on Mentoring," *Journal of Music Teacher Education* 8, no. 2 (1999): 7–13.

8. American Federation of Teachers, "Beginning Teacher Induction: The Essential Bridge," *Educational Issues Policy Brief,* no. 13 (2001); Linda Darling-Hammond, "Keeping Good Teachers: Why It Matters, What Leaders Can Do," *Educational Leadership* 60, no. 8 (2003): 6–13; Yvonne Gold, "Beginning Teacher Support: Attrition, Mentoring and Induction," in *Handbook of Research on Teacher Education,* ed. J. Sikula, 2nd ed. (New York: Macmillan, 1996), 548–94; National Association of State Boards of Education (NASBE), *The Numbers Game: Ensuring Quantity and Quality in the Teaching Work Force* (Alexandria, VA: NASBE, 1998); National Commission on Teaching and America's Future (NCTAF), *No Dream Denied: A Pledge to America's Children* (New York: Author, 2003); Barry Sweeney, "A Survey of the 50 State-Mandated Novice Teacher Programs: Implications for State and Local Mentoring Programs and Practices," 1998. Unpublished manuscript available from http://www.teacher-mentors.com.

9. Gary A. Griffin, "Teacher Induction: Research Issues," *Journal of Teacher Education* 36, no. 1, (1985): 42–46; Ralph Kester and Mary Marockie, "Local Induction Programs," in *Teacher Induction—A New Beginning* (Reston, VA: Association of Teacher Educators, 1987), 25–30; Katherine Perez, Carole Swain, and Carolyn Hartsough, "An Analysis of Practices Used to Support New Teachers," *Teacher Education Quarterly* 24, no. 2 (1997): 41–52; New Teacher Center, *Continuum of Teacher Development* (Santa Cruz, CA: Author, 2002).

10. Feiman-Nemser et al., *A Conceptual Review of Literature on New Teacher Induction;* Gary A. Griffin, ed., *The Education of Teachers. Ninety-Eighth Yearbook of the National Society for the Study of Education* (Chicago: University of Chicago Press, 1999); Marge Scherer, ed., *A Better Beginning: Supporting and Mentoring New Teachers* (Alexandria, VA: Association for Supervision and Curriculum Development, 1999); "Keeping Good Teachers," [Special Focus Issue] *Educational Leadership* 60, no. 8 (2003).

11. Colleen M. Conway, Patti J. Krueger, Mitchell Robinson, Paul Haack, and Michael V.

Smith, "Beginning Music Teacher Induction and Mentor Policies: A Cross-state Perspective," *Arts Education Policy Review* 104, no. 2, (2002): 9–18.

12. Conway, "Beginning Music Teacher Perceptions of District-sponsored Induction Programs"; DeLorenzo, "Perceived Problems of Beginning Music Teachers"; Krueger, "New Music Teachers Speak out on Mentoring."

13. Feiman-Nemser et al., *A Conceptual Review of Literature on New Teacher Induction*, 2.

14. Consortium of National Arts Education Associations, *National Standards for Arts Education* (Reston, VA: MENC, 1994).

15. Feiman-Nemser et al., *A Conceptual Review of Literature on New Teacher Induction*, 4.

16. Conway, "Beginning Music Teacher Perceptions of District-sponsored Induction Programs"; DeLorenzo, "Perceived Problems of Beginning Music Teachers"; Krueger, "New Music Teachers Speak out on Mentoring."

17. Feiman-Nemser et al., *A Conceptual Review of Literature on New Teacher Induction*, 4–5.

18. Ibid., 3.

Colleen M. Conway is assistant professor of music education at the University of Michigan School of Music.

School District-Sponsored Induction Programs

Colleen M. Conway

Before we can consider ways in which the music education profession can assist the beginning music teacher through induction support, it is important to understand the typical experiences of music teachers in school district-sponsored induction programs. The experiences of music teachers described in this section are true accounts.[1] All names have been changed, but the situations are real. As you read these short accounts notice (a) the teaching schedules and preparation given to these beginning teachers, (b) the extracurricular expectations, (c) issues of communication between teachers and administrators, (d) when induction programs began in relation to when the teachers needed assistance, and (e) the overall level of teacher satisfaction with the district-sponsored programs.

BRIAN

Brian teaches in a small, rural district. His schedule includes beginning band at the elementary school, sixth-grade general music, sixth-grade band, and a seventh- and eighth-grade band in the middle school, a high school choir class, high school jazz band, and assisting with high school band and marching band. He assisted with band camp and a number of summer parades before the start of this school year. Brian's seventh- and eighth-grade ensembles attended the state band and orchestra festival in the spring. His district paid for him to attend a county-sponsored beginning teacher induction program that included eight day-long sessions for new teachers. A substitute was hired to teach his classes while he attended the workshops. These workshops focused on general classroom management and instructional strategies (including cooperative learning, questioning strategies, assessment of student learning, and achievement test preparation).

Brian did not attend the first of his eight induction meetings because he did not know about it. After it had occurred his principal asked, "How was the induction meeting?" and Brian replied, "What induction meeting?" The principal responded with an apology for not letting Brian know about the program. Brian did attend the second induction meeting. In reflecting on his experience, he says: "We spent a lot of time on cooperative learning techniques. It felt a little like one of my teacher education classes in college. It was pretty hard to figure out how to relate it to a band setting." Brian planned to attend the third induction meeting, but the other band director in the school who was supposed to substitute for him got sick so Brian had to stay and teach his own classes as well as his colleague's. Brian attended the fourth, fifth, sixth, seventh, and eighth meeting. However, he suggested that by missing the first meeting he always felt a little behind. He said some of the classroom management strategies discussed were useful, but again, it was sometimes difficult to transfer content from the workshops to a music setting. Brian also commented that it was very hard to miss rehearsals every other Wednesday as he was preparing his ensembles for the state competition: "I would just rather stay back and work with my kids."

MARIE

Marie teaches K–5 general music in a large, suburban district. She sees her students once per week for forty minutes and travels between two buildings in the district. There is no music room in either building, so Marie travels to each classroom with a music cart. She participated in a beginning teacher induction program that was provided for all beginning teachers in the county (a different county program from Brian's). She was required by contract to attend five after-school meetings for new teachers. The sessions focused on classroom management and instructional strategies. Marie was extremely dissatisfied with the induction meetings and felt that they did not relate to her work as a traveling music teacher: "I got pretty disgusted. I don't like wasting time." Marie is often confused about the requirements of the program and is not sure who to talk to about her induction work. This confusion is compounded by her work in multiple buildings and the apparent lack of communication between building administrators about her.

TOM

Tom teaches fifth- through eighth-grade band in a large, suburban district. His fifth-grade class includes more than one hundred beginning instrumental students in a room designed for a maximum of eighty. Although the high school director had been available to assist in the fifth-grade class early in the school year, once marching season was over Tom had to work with these fifth-grade students by himself. In addition, he has a sixth-grade band, a seventh-grade band, and an eighth-grade band that meet every day. He assisted with band camp in the summer, with marching band in the evenings, and at football games throughout the fall semester. His seventh- and eighth-grade bands participated in the state band and orchestra festival, and he prepared many of the middle school students for participation in the state solo and ensemble competition. He participated in the beginning teacher induction program that was required of all beginning teachers in the county. Tom felt that these programs really did not get at the issues that were problematic for him: "How do you manage a class of one hundred beginning instrumentalists who do not have any skills and yet are meeting all together for 'band'?" He said when he did ask the instructors questions about his setting, the response was usually, "I really don't know anything about music."

ALLISON

Allison teaches K–3 general music in two elementary buildings in a large, urban district. She sees her classes once a week for thirty minutes. Some of her classes meet on the stage at the school. For other classes she travels to classrooms with a cart. Her district provided a beginning teacher induction program that was presented as an optional program for beginning teachers. The program was offered on Monday afternoons and included workshops on classroom management and district contract issues. The program in Allison's district did not start until well into the school year. By the time it began, Allison had already committed to teaching classes in the community music school and could not attend any of the sessions. She commented: "I would have happily attended the induction meetings, but I could not back out on the community music school."

JAMES

James teaches in a small, rural district. His teaching schedule includes beginning band at the elementary school, sixth-grade band, junior high band (seventh and eighth grade), high school choir, high school band, and marching band. In addition, James prepared his students for participation in the state solo and ensemble competition and took his junior high and high school bands to the state band and orchestra competition. There was no induction program in James's district. James's principal commented: "It's just great how the state comes down from above and tells us to provide an induction program. How are we supposed to pay for that? We have a very strong teacher's union here and we would have to pay teachers to attend if it happened outside of school. Small districts like this one will never be able to provide support unless the state gives us money."

TRISH

Trish teaches sixth-, seventh-, and eighth-grade band in a large, urban middle school. Trish sees her students for a ninety-minute rehearsal every day. Trish took her seventh- and eighth-grade bands to the state band and orchestra festival, and she prepared many of the students for participation in the state solo and ensemble festival. There was no induction program in Trish's district. Her principal suggested: "I think the higher education folks should be more involved with this phase of teacher education. A large urban district like this has too many other things to worry about." Trish suggested that in addition to general beginning music teacher issues, she needed a focus on urban schools that the district was unable to provide.

TEACHERS ARE DISSATISFIED WITH
DISTRICT-SPONSORED PROGRAMS

All of the teachers described above who attended induction programs were dissatisfied with the programs. They were already overwhelmed by their first-year teaching responsibilities, and the induction program did not provide them with a place to work through the problems they were experiencing. Although experienced teachers may look at the content of these programs (classroom management and instructional strategies) and deem them valuable, the beginning teachers did not view them as valuable. Regardless of the potential value of the content, the induction programs were not helpful to these teachers.

MUSIC TEACHERS NEED INDUCTION SUPPORT
BEFORE SCHOOLS STARTS

The timing of the induction programs was also problematic for these music teachers. Many of them began working with students early in the summer in band camps. James said, "I needed help from day one. Day one was in August for me." Allison was unable to attend her program because information about the program was circulated too late. Marie had to miss several of her programs due to previous commitments. Music teachers typically are busy people. Programs for them must accommodate this lifestyle.

MUSIC TEACHERS HAVE DIFFICULT TEACHING
SCHEDULES AND ENVIRONMENTS

Much of the general teacher education literature suggests that beginning teachers are often given the most difficult assignments.[2] Brian and James had to prepare for multiple classes including fifth- through twelfth-grade instrumental music and teach in at least two different buildings. Brian and James also had to prepare for high school choral music, and Brian had elementary general music as well. Marie and Allison were both in multiple buildings, teaching a variety of grade levels and traveling from class to class with a music cart. Tom had more students in his fifth-grade band than he had chairs in the band room. Trish saw adolescent children in an urban school for ninety minutes at a time. All of the instrumental music teachers had tremendous responsibilities for marching band in the fall, festival competitions in the spring, and solo and ensemble preparations.

Many music teachers begin their careers in smaller school districts that need one music teacher to do a variety of musical things that they may or may not be prepared to do. The principals of the schools where these new teachers taught all agreed that the job description of the music teacher is an awesome one. However, there were no suggestions from administrators about how to change this. I believe music teachers being expected to have full and diverse teaching schedules is a part of the culture of music education in general. As music educators, we spend a great deal of time justifying our very existence in the curriculum. Yet, if teachers are given schedules that are completely unreasonable, we can never get to the point where the aesthetic value of music can even be discovered.

MUSIC TEACHERS ARE BUSY "MUSICIANS" OUTSIDE OF SCHOOL

Music teachers are often active in the musical community outside of school. Lisa DeLorenzo documented that "finding time to continue own musical growth" was one of the most cited frustrations of the beginning music teacher.[3] All the music teachers discussed in this chapter were musically active outside of their school teaching responsibilities: Brian was singing in a local community choir and teaching private music lessons, Marie was teaching private voice lessons and working with a church choir, James was teaching private music lessons, Allison was teaching early childhood music in a community music center and working with a youth choir at church, Tom was teaching private music lessons and playing in a local community orchestra, and Trish was teaching private music lessons. These outside musical responsibilities often conflicted with teachers' abilities to participate in induction programs in the districts that had them. It is important for music teachers to stay connected to the musical community and for designers of induction programs for beginning music teachers to be aware of these potential scheduling conflicts.

ISSUES OF RETENTION

Brian, James, and Tom are no longer teaching in the districts where they began. Trish, Allison, and Marie continue to talk about moving. The transient nature of music teaching presents a challenge for induction. Districts are hesitant to spend money on teachers who may leave the district. This is especially true in small, rural schools that are used to a high turnover rate among music teachers.

NOTES

1. The beginning music teacher profiles presented in this chapter first appeared in Colleen M. Conway, "Beginning Music Teacher Perceptions of District-sponsored Induction Programs," *Bulletin of the Council for Research in Music Education,* no. 151 (2001): 1–11. Reprinted with permission.

2. Sharon Feiman-Nemser, "What New Teachers Need to Learn," *Educational Leadership* 60, no. 8 (2003): 25–29; Sharon Feiman-Nemser, Sharon Schwille, Cindy Carver, and Brian Yusko, *A Conceptual Review of Literature on New Teacher Induction* (E. Lansing, MI: National Partnership of Excellence and Accountability in Teaching [NPEAT], 1999), Document #Ed449147, Sponsored by the Office of Educational Research and Improvement, Washington, DC; Gary A. Griffin, ed., *The Education of Teachers. Ninety-Eighth Yearbook of the National Society for the Study of Education* (Chicago: University of Chicago Press, 1999); Leslie Huling-Austin, "Teacher Induction Programs and Internships," in *Handbook of Research in Teacher Education* (New York: Macmillan, 1990), 535–48; Leslie Huling-Austin, "Research on Learning to Teach: Implications for Teacher Induction and Mentoring Programs," *Journal of Teacher Education* 43, no. 3 (1992): 163–72; Leslie Huling-Austin, *Becoming a Teacher: What Research Tells Us* (Indianapolis, IN: Kappa Delta Pi Publications, 1994).

3. Lisa DeLorenzo, "Perceived Problems of Beginning Music Teachers," *Bulletin of the Council for Research in Music Education,* no. 113 (1992): 9–25.

Colleen M. Conway is assistant professor of music education at the University of Michigan School of Music.

State-Sponsored Induction Programs

Mitchell Robinson and Patti J. Krueger

CONNECTICUT'S BEGINNING EDUCATOR SUPPORT AND TRAINING (BEST) PROGRAM

Mitchell Robinson

Background and Context

Since the mid-1980s, the state of Connecticut's educational reform agenda has focused on promoting high standards for students and teachers. The Education Enhancement Act of 1986 was highly successful in raising standards for teacher education and licensing, upgrading professional development programs, and increasing teacher salaries to levels competitive with other professions. This linking of higher teacher salaries to increased professional standards has been effective in attracting more academically qualified educators to Connecticut's schools.[1]

These initiatives also led to a new three-tiered certification system, which consists of the following components:[2]

Initial Educator Certificate

- Valid for three years.
- Candidate must then complete BEST and accrue ten months' experience before becoming eligible for a Provisional Certificate.

Provisional Educator Certificate

- Valid for eight years.
- Candidate must then complete thirty graduate credits or a master's degree and accrue thirty months' experience before becoming eligible for a Professional Certificate.

41

Professional Educator Certificate

- Valid for five years.
- Candidate must then complete nine CEUs or six graduate credits every five years to remain certified.

In order to be eligible for the Provisional Educator Certificate, beginning teachers must demonstrate mastery of essential teaching competencies related to content knowledge, planning, instruction, and assessment. These competencies are assessed through the portfolio assessment component of the Beginning Educator Support and Training Program, a comprehensive three-year teacher induction program. The BEST Program provides

- Support for beginning teachers through school- or district-based mentors or support teams and through state-sponsored training such as portfolio clinics, beginning teacher seminars, and other forms of professional development.
- Assessment through a discipline-specific teaching portfolio submitted during the second year of teaching, in which beginning teachers document a unit of instruction around important concepts or goals in a series of lessons, assess student learning, and reflect on their students' learning and the quality of their teaching. The portfolio includes session logs, videotapes of teaching, examples of student work and student assessments, and teacher commentaries.

Drawing from initiatives at the national level, the Connecticut State Department of Education piloted a portfolio assessment program of beginning teachers in 1996 to replace the system of classroom observations that had been in place. In 2000, the state required all second-year teachers to complete this portfolio assessment, with the provision that those who failed be given a third year to complete the assessment and receive a provisional certificate. The Music Education content area went on-line in 2002, meaning that from then on teachers who do not successfully complete the portfolio assessment by the end of their third year of service are denied licensure.

Induction and Support in the BEST Program

During the summer of 2001, trained portfolio assessors (primarily practicing teachers and university professors) at the Connecticut Department of Education evaluated more than two thousand portfolios (approximately seventy-five of these were music teacher portfolios). Out of the two thousand teachers who submitted portfolios, approximately 85 percent received passing grades.

Portfolios are graded on a scale of one to four, with four being the highest possible score; a score of two or higher is needed to pass. Those who score below two have another chance to submit a portfolio in their third year. If that attempt is also unsatisfactory, they are no longer candidates for certification. Among the factors considered in the portfolio assessment are beginning teachers' abilities to plan and implement instruction, evaluate student learning and analyze their own teaching, know their students, and adapt instruction for individual students.

State funding for the BEST Program has evolved from a high of $10.2 million in 1990–91 to $3.0 million in 1991–92. At that time, state funds for mentor stipends were eliminated. Program funding has remained at approximately $3.2 million per year over the last ten years, although the State Board of Education has repeatedly supported the restoration of state funding for mentor stipends. It should be noted that, during this period, the state continued to provide local districts with professional development funds that districts could use to support mandated released time for mentors and beginning teachers to meet with one another as well as to fund professional development activities. Projected state budget shortfalls in 2002–03 may result in the elimination of the professional development funds during that fiscal year. However, districts may use new and expanded Title II teacher quality funds to pay stipends for mentors, support released time for teachers, and pay for teacher professional development activities. The state also provides compensation to districts for released time of up to four visitation days per year for each beginning teacher and compensates mentors during their first year of involvement with the program.

Perhaps due to the small size of the state, the experience in Connecticut with respect to communication between the school music education community and state policy makers has been an unusually positive one. From the very beginning, policy discussions have been conducted by teams of practicing teachers, university personnel, and state education department officials.

The BEST program's administrative structure reinforces this inclusive approach to policy generation. Each content or certification area is led by a team consisting of a Teacher-in-Residence (TIR), a Scholar-in-Residence (SIR), and a subject area consultant. The members of the team report to a bureau chief in the State Department of Education (SDE), who is responsible for the BEST program in all content areas.

The TIR typically is a veteran public school teacher on special assignment for a period of two years. This person is released from his or her home school district duties four days per week; the SDE "buys" the TIR's contract, allowing the home school district to hire a replacement teacher during the length of the assignment. TIRs are experienced teachers who are recognized as leaders by their peers and their colleagues in higher education. Many TIRs also serve as project leaders for their content areas, organizing and administrating all necessary duties, tasks, and activities.

The SIR usually is a university professor who specializes in the preparation of teachers in the content area. These individuals work as part-time independent consultants, devoting approximately one day per week during the academic year to BEST-related duties. The SIR's main responsibilities are to provide the theoretical framework for the discussions regarding assessment strategies and instructional content in the certification area, to facilitate the training of portfolio scorers and trainers, and to supervise, along with the TIRs, the summer portfolio scoring institute. SIRs also serve as important curricular links to collegiate teacher preparation programs, ensuring that what is expected of beginning teachers in the BEST program is actually being addressed in undergraduate courses and curricula.

The subject area consultant is a full-time SDE employee who serves as a curriculum specialist in each given content area. These individuals not only serve as important liaisons between the SDE and the rest of the BEST leadership team but also provide valuable professional guidance during all parts of the process. The leadership team is directly responsible for coordinating the work of practicing teachers who serve as seminar leaders, new scorer trainers, and portfolio scorers. Depending on content area, anywhere from twenty to three hundred teachers function in these roles during the academic year and the summer scoring institute, not to mention the contributions of veteran teachers who serve as mentors for novices each year.

During the 2001–02 academic year the BEST music leadership team met on a regular basis (approximately ten to fifteen hours per semester) to develop strategies for selecting and training scorers, refining evaluation tools and procedures, and designing and implementing professional development seminars for beginning teachers. Communication among team members is frequent and substantive and is conducted via e-mail, phone conversations, written correspondence, and face-to-face meetings. The members of the music leadership team have developed a deep sense of mutual respect for one another based on the recognition of each member's professional perspective and contributions to the group. Perhaps the greatest strength of the Connecticut model is the collaboration of professionals from multiple components of the state's music education community—public schools, higher education, and the state department of education—in an effort to work towards a shared mission and a common goal: "to improve the quality of the state's teaching workforce by supporting teachers in the critical induction years and providing opportunities for experienced educators to serve in the roles of mentors and assessors."[3]

Support for beginning teachers is ongoing and comprehensive, but optional—licensure candidates are encouraged but not required to take advantage of the series of professional development opportunities specifically designed for them as a part of the BEST Program. The BEST Support Seminar Series includes two on-site regional seminars and four additional online distance-learning seminars. The on-site seminars provide beginning teachers with opportunities for interaction and collegial exchange with beginning teachers and with the experienced teachers who conduct the seminars. The online seminars are designed to improve access to important professional development information for beginning teachers and to facilitate collaboration between beginning teachers and their mentors or content colleagues.

Each of the four online seminars includes six sections:

- *Lessons* provide a review of one or more components of effective teaching in the beginning teacher's discipline or area. The lesson provides the framework needed to participate fully in the seminar.
- *Exercises* are activities designed to assist beginning teachers in focusing on important elements of effective teaching in their discipline. They are directly related to the lesson content within each seminar. Many are designed to facilitate focused interactions and collaborative work between beginning teachers and their mentors or content colleagues. Answering the focus questions in the exercises will help beginning teachers reflect on their own teaching and assist them in preparing for the portfolio requirement.
- The *Conference* is an opportunity to post responses to seminar exercises, read the postings of other beginning teachers, and read the seminar leader's response, which contains summary information about patterns and trends identified in the postings.
- The *Portfolio Corner* identifies the direct link between the content of each seminar and the portfolio requirement.
- The *Mentor Corner* includes key issues or questions that a beginning teacher and his or her mentor or content colleague can use to focus discussions on effective teaching.
- *Resources* include discipline-specific standards, actual portfolio samples, related recommended Web sites, and more. In some cases, beginning teachers must refer to the resources in order to complete the seminar exercises.[4]

The content of the BEST Support Seminar Series focuses on the "Three Artistic Processes," Connecticut's streamlined version of the National Standards for Music Education.[5] The Three Artistic Processes (Creating, Performing, and Responding) were originally outlined in the *NAEP 1997 Arts Education Assessment Framework*.[6] They form the core of the BEST Program's assessment criteria, encouraging beginning teachers to design, implement, assess, and reflect on authentic activities in music making and study and to actively engage their students in such activities. Due to the complex, complicated nature of music teaching and learning, the processes are conceived as being integrated (see

45

Figure 1). For example, rather than asking beginning teachers to design isolated lessons and activities for each of the processes, candidates are encouraged to demonstrate an appropriate balance of learning activities in creating, performing, and responding over the course of a series of instructional sequences. This issue of balance is stressed in both the BEST Support Seminar Series and in the training of assessors, creating a model of reflective practice that is powerful and relevant for beginning music teachers and experienced assessors alike.

FIGURE 1. THE THREE ARTISTIC PROCESSES: ANOTHER PERSPECTIVE. THIS GRAPHIC ILLUSTRATES THE INTEGRATED NATURE OF THE ARTISTIC PROCESS IN ACTION.

CREATING

Imagining
- Developing idea(s) (concepts, ideas, feelings)

Planning
- Experimenting, researching, and designing ways of presenting idea(s) through artistic materials

Making, Evaluating, Refining
- Applying knowledge and skills/techniques to bring idea(s) to life through artistic work
- Evaluating quality and refining successive versions ("drafts") of the work

Presenting
- Presenting in performance or exhibiting completed work for others

PERFORMING

Selecting
- Choosing an artistic work (repertoire) to perform

Analyzing
- Analyzing structure and researching background of work

Interpreting
- Developing a personal interpretation of work (an idea of its expressive intent or potential)

Rehearsing, Evaluating, Refining
- Applying knowledge and skills/technique to bring personal interpretation to life through performance
- Evaluating quality and refining successive versions of the performance

Presenting
- Performing work for others

STANDARDS-BASED MUSIC TEACHING

RESPONDING

Selecting
- Choosing an artistic work and/or performance to experience

Analyzing
- Seeing/hearing and comprehending visual/aural features of the work and performance
- Mentally assembling what is seen/heard into a whole

Interpreting
- Developing a personal response to (constructing meaning from) the expressive ideas of both the creator(s) and performer(s)

Evaluating
- Evaluating quality of artistic work and the performance

Note. Graphic developed by N. Carlotta Parr, after content developed by Scott Shuler. Copyright © 2000 by the Connecticut State Board of Education in the name of the Secretary of the State of Connecticut. Reprinted with permission.

Implications

While political realities and local policies and procedures make each situation unique, there are characteristics of the Connecticut model that can provide valuable information for music education leaders planning similar beginning music teacher evaluation initiatives in their areas. It is important to remember, however, that for an initiative like this to be considered truly successful, it must be designed specifically for your own area. It should go without saying that beginning music teacher assessment is definitely not an "off the shelf" or "one size fits all" proposition.

Communication and collaboration. The BEST Program has been in existence since 1996 and is in a process of nearly continuous revision. Team leaders, portfolio assessors, and beginning teachers are constantly queried in an effort to improve and refine the procedures in place to gather data, construct rubric language, and make evaluative decisions. Critical to this open design structure are the contributions from individuals from many parts of Connecticut's school music community—state department officials, collegiate music teacher education faculty members, and practicing PreK–12 music teachers. In research terms, obtaining feedback and perspective from all of these various "stakeholders" provides a sort of "data triangulation" that helps to ensure the internal validity or trustworthiness of the assessment process. Pragmatically, it just makes good sense for everyone involved in school music to be on the same page when it comes to such an important issue that affects music teaching and learning in our state.

Mentor and assessor training. Unlike similar programs in other states,[7] the BEST Program requires that all mentors and assessors undergo a rigorous and comprehensive training program that includes a discipline-specific training component. Training is conducted by state department officials, collegiate teacher education faculty members, and other team leaders. Both mentors and portfolio scorers are selected through a rigorous application process, and must be nominated by their school districts.

Each portfolio scorer must complete at least fifty hours of comprehensive, discipline-specific training in the scoring of portfolios and meet a predetermined proficiency standard prior to scoring portfolios. The commitment for portfolio scorers includes "completing all components of the initial scorer training and the proficiency process, scoring for three years as a portfolio scorer (need not be consecutive years), and participating in refresher training and proficiency testing after year one."[8] Portfolio scorers are compensated $100 per completed portfolio and receive a $300 stipend for completing both required training and proficiency scoring activities.[9] Involvement in the BEST Program is having profound effects on the veteran teachers who serve as portfolio scorers, especially in terms of building confidence and encouraging teachers to become more reflective practitioners.

Discipline-specific mentor matching. While our colleagues in general education maintain that the most important criterion for good mentor-mentee matches is having both partners working in the same building, current research in music education suggests that the content area (music-music) match is a far more powerful predictor of success for the novice. My experience in Connecticut has reinforced this premise. In a study of beginning music teachers, I identified the following types of mentors that were mentioned in my interviews with novice teachers:

Formal
Building mentor: assigned at the school level, usually not from the same subject area; helps with school-level and district procedures and policies/politics.

BEST mentor: assigned by the district; assists with BEST program questions and portfolio issues; often not music-related.

Informal
Beginning Teacher (BT) buddy: another newly-hired teacher, either in the same subject area or not; someone to commiserate with, confide in; often from the beginning teacher's own building or district or former college classmates.

Subject-area mentor: rarely assigned by the school; an experienced colleague who happens to teach the same subject and can offer guidance or serve as a sounding board.

Respected elder: someone who has subject area knowledge and experience and a vested interest in the beginning teacher; includes former cooperating teachers, a current assistant principal who had been the previous high school band director in that building and "knew the ropes," or former professors.

Of these various types of mentors, the novice teachers in my study identified the *subject-area mentors* and the *respected elders* as being most helpful to their growth as music teachers. While the other, nonmusic mentors on the list often were valued for their "insider" knowledge of the school culture (i.e., how to operate the copier, where to get coffee in the morning, etc.), the novices clearly relied on the two music mentor types for their questions about music teaching, student learning, and curricular issues.

This finding has also been reinforced through discussions with beginning teachers in Connecticut Music Educators Association-sponsored roundtables at the state's annual in-service conference. These sessions, organized and coordinated by Jeanne D'Angelo, the BEST Teacher-in-Residence for Music, have been presented at the state conference for each of the past few years and provide an excellent avenue into the thoughts and perspectives of beginning music teachers. A common theme at these sessions has been the value placed on having a music teacher assigned as a mentor. Again and again, these novice educators testified to the importance of pairing veteran music teachers with less experienced colleagues and sang the praises of having a fellow music teacher as a mentor.

Discipline-specific assessment. Another strength of the BEST model is its adoption of discipline-specific assessment standards. That is to say, music teachers are assessed using music criteria, and math teachers are assessed using math criteria, instead of using generic teaching standards applied uniformly across disciplines. Connecticut is currently the only state to provide this sort of discipline-specific evaluation program for beginning teachers.

While this approach requires numbers of well-trained portfolio assessors in each specific content area, the benefits have outweighed the disadvantages in music education. For example, there is now a large supply of experienced music teacher evaluators in the state, many of whom have moved into leadership roles in their home school districts as music supervisors, teacher leaders, and administrators. These individuals function as articulate, well-informed advocates for music's importance as a discipline worthy of study in Connecticut's schools, strengthening the leadership structure in music statewide.

Benefits for veteran teachers. Even after rotating out of active involvement with the BEST Program, many of these individuals become valuable resources within their home schools and across the state. Armed with the knowledge and confidence gained from working as assessors of beginning music teachers, these veteran educators often move on to serve as mentors for beginning teachers or are asked to provide training for prospective mentors.

The impact of this work on the assessors themselves has been profound. In the words of the assessors:

- "I am ten times more confident in myself as a teacher ... as a direct result of my involvement with the BEST program."
- "I have begun to incorporate more aspects of our definition of good teaching into my own practice—have also been able to articulate qualities of good practice to the teachers that I supervise."
- "Somehow word spreads quickly about involvement with BEST; for two years in a row I have been asked to consult and proofread portfolios for elementary classroom teachers—although the task is different, I feel confident in my ability to offer advice."
- "My role as a table leader has had the biggest impact on my professional growth—up until now, I felt that my poor teaching situation would make for a bad environment for a student teacher—I realize now, however, that in spite of a crazy schedule, I have much I could and should be sharing with new music teachers."
- "Five years ago I would have said 'What Three Artistic Processes?'; now, my students create some, respond some—before, music education was mainly

49

about 'making music' mainly through performance—I would not be teaching this way now but for my involvement with BEST."[10]

It is clear from these comments, and many others like them, that these teachers have been strongly affected by their involvement in the BEST Program. While we often look at the impact that these sorts of initiatives have on beginning teachers, it may be that the strongest reasons for examining such programs will be to determine their influence on veteran teachers. It is often said that one of the prime reasons that teachers identify for leaving the profession is a "lack of space to grow." Perhaps getting involved in beginning teacher assessment initiatives is one of the means through which our more experienced colleagues can find the room to grow without leaving the classroom entirely.

WASHINGTON'S TEACHER ASSISTANCE PROGRAM
Patti J. Krueger

Since 1987, school districts in Washington state have had the opportunity to apply each school year for state funding under Washington's Teacher Assistance Program (TAP) to help their beginning teachers make the transition into the profession. Participating districts agree to assign an experienced, exemplary teacher to mentor each new teacher, to provide training to the mentor and the beginning teacher, and to allow both teachers to observe each other and other teachers. Districts provide an orientation prior to the school year, assistance throughout the school year, and assistance in the development of a professional growth plan for the new teacher. State funding is to be used for mentor and beginning teacher stipends, training, released time for observations, and other assistance to allow mentors and new teachers time to observe each other and to provide guided experience and planning.

Participation is not mandatory, and Washington TAP coordinators believe that participation is now close to but not yet at 100 percent for districts that have first-year teachers. For the 2001–02 school year, the Washington legislature allotted $1,400 to districts for each new teacher's assistance costs. Districts may apply to use TAP funds to assist second-year and more experienced teachers who request a mentor. Districts apply for participation through Washington's Supervisor of Public Instruction Office.[11] Optional mentor workshops are offered throughout Washington each summer to assist and prepare mentors.

Washington's Teacher Assistance Program provides a variety of tools and resources for new teachers and mentors to use and integrates many research findings into its guidelines for mentoring. Guidelines for lesson planning, observations, teaching strategies, monitoring student learning, motivating students, and working with students who have special needs are provided and suggested on the TAP Web site.[12] Mentor responsibilities include modeling effective strategies in their own classrooms and observing new teachers with follow-up meetings for feedback and planning. Mentors are asked to guide new teachers in areas such as classroom management, student discipline, curriculum, instructional and communication skills, assessment, professional conduct, incorporating the state's essential academic learning requirements into instructional plans, and raising the achievement of students of diverse learning styles and backgrounds.

All districts participating in Washington's TAP are required to include collaboration with school principals who supervise new teachers. Principals are asked to learn about the mentoring process and support both mentors and new teachers. Because new teachers are often concerned about formal evaluation, TAP mentors are asked to maintain confidentiality about their observations and conferences. TAP guidelines suggest that mentors may share a list of topics discussed with administrators but not their perceptions of the beginning teacher's effectiveness. Accordingly, mentors do not formally evaluate the beginning teachers with whom they work.

Professional Growth Plan and Certification

The Teacher Assistance Program also asks mentors to provide support, materials, and guidance for new teachers to complete a professional growth plan. Beginning with teachers certified in 2001, this plan is the first step in completing the continuing Professional Certificate, which Washington State teachers are required to apply for after they complete their first five years of teaching. A professional growth plan for beginning teachers contains a description of evidence showing that the candidate meets specific standards for effective teaching, professional development, and leadership. The plan reflects the candidate's teaching context and requires that the new teacher provide portfolio evidence demonstrating a positive impact of his or her teaching on student learning.

In order to complete a professional growth plan for continuing professional certification, new teachers are asked to form a support team of three members, including a colleague chosen by the candidate, a representative from the candidate's school district, and a college or university advisor. New teachers begin by identifying their own strengths and challenges from the criteria required for continuing professional certification. Mentor teachers assist in clarifying which criteria need most attention based on their classroom observations. The new teacher's principal, supervisor, or other team members might also suggest areas needing attention. The new teacher chooses several criteria to focus on and shares these with the mentor for observation purposes. Over the course of their first five school years, new teachers can complete the professional growth planning process for continuing certification. This new certification process will be initially assessed in 2006 as the first teachers complete the new requirements.

In summary, Washington's Teacher Assistance Program provides mentor support and training, guidelines, and materials to assist new teachers. Guidance is also provided to aid the new teacher in completing a professional growth plan required for the Professional Certification process in Washington.

Washington Teacher Assistance Program Assessment

The Washington Teacher Assistance Program has established the following goals for participating districts:

- using specially trained, carefully selected mentors to assist new teachers
- providing scheduled and structured time for mentors and new teachers to work together
- providing training to groups of new teachers on topics that relate directly to their needs and developmental stage
- having mentors follow up to ensure that new teachers are using new skills effectively in their classrooms

Program goals also recommend that a mentor's content and grade-level expertise match that of the novice and that mentor training include a component on observation and conferencing strategies.[13]

TAP coordinators acknowledge that school districts throughout Washington state are meeting program goals to varying degrees. Some districts are employing full-time district or building mentors, while other districts are not yet consistently providing training or guidelines to mentors. In response to this problem, program improvements have focused on offering assistance to districts in program planning and implementation and on eliciting feedback from partici-pants. Beginning teachers are now surveyed each year about the types and effectiveness of assistance they receive, and districts are provided with this information. Implementation challenges have been greatest for small and remote districts, and TAP program coordinators encourage small districts to look outside of their districts for mentor teachers when needed. The program has proposed but has not yet been granted funds for several regional coordinators who could travel to more remote districts to provide support with program design, training, and mentoring.[14]

How is the Teacher Assistance Program impacting Washington State's novice music teachers? I found varying degrees of participation between districts when I interviewed (for this chapter) a small sample of new music teachers from five school districts about the effectiveness of the assistance they received. Mentors in some districts were more consistently viewed as effective and well-prepared to help novice teachers than in other districts. In some districts, novice music teachers noted that their mentors held teaching positions in areas and levels of music different from their own, making them less able to provide specific help where needed. New music teachers in some districts noted that mentors seemed to have little or no mentor guidance or training. One first-year music teacher illustrated this situation:

> All the new teachers in our district have been assigned a mentor, but I don't think the mentors have been trained at all. My mentor called in December and said that they told her she was my mentor, so if I needed anything to let her know. Neither of us really knew how to go about it, so that was pretty much it! It would really help if the district expectations for mentors were made clear. (First-year orchestra teacher, Interview 9)

In this particular district, mentors and new teachers did not seem to be aware of available guidelines or mentor training provided by the Washington TAP program. Though mentors were available and willing, new teachers did not feel that effective support was provided.

In contrast, several of the new music teachers interviewed were quite satisfied with and appreciated the mentoring provided in their district. One novice music teacher who had a positive mentoring experience noted:

> I've been working in parallel with my mentor who is an experienced elementary music teacher. She has been a great resource. We've shared lesson plans, and my first program was very similar to hers. Now I'm branching out and doing more of my own thing. My mentor was a great role model for curriculum and management, especially during the first few weeks of school. (First-year general music teacher, Interview 3)

Another stated:

> My mentor met with me extensively before the school year began and weekly for the first three months of school. We went over lesson plans and talked about issues that came up in my classroom. He helped me to analyze why something didn't go well and what to try doing about it. This really helped me to see what and how and why a master teacher does what he does ... to understand the difference between what kindergartners versus first graders can understand and do, and how to write a sequential curriculum. I can't imagine what my first year would have been like if I hadn't had a mentor who was an experienced music teacher! Much of my success this year is due to my mentor teacher's work with me. (First-year general music teacher, Interview 7)

These new Washington music teachers were among several interviewed who found their mentor experiences very effective in a variety of ways during the first year of teaching. Guidance in building a sequential, yearlong curriculum, in analyzing classroom problems, and in establishing a system of discipline and management was noted as particularly helpful.

New music teachers often spoke of observing other teachers during the first year as a great resource. One teacher described her experience:

> Our district allows one visit out of the building by the new teacher, and one visit by the mentor into the building. I did my visit at another middle school band classroom, and that was very valuable. I'd like to do more visits. (First-year band teacher, Interview 6)

As illustrated here, new music teachers interviewed most often felt that observations of other music teachers were valuable and that they would have benefitted from several more than the number allowed by their district. Some districts sampled allowed for only one released observation, while others allowed up to three full days released time for new music teachers to observe other teachers.

The ideas behind the Washington TAP program were consistently seen as positive by the new music teachers interviewed, and some districts were viewed by their new teachers as providing very effective first-year teacher support. The elements of the program that new music teachers valued most were the opportunity to meet regularly with mentors in similar music teaching positions prior to and during the first few months of school and opportunities to observe experienced music teachers in the classroom. Some novices also spoke highly of districtwide seminars for first-year teachers.

In contrast, the level of support provided was minimal and sporadic in other Washington districts sampled. Anecdotes (such as those preceding) reinforced TAP data showing that a wide variation exists between programs from one district to the next. Some district programs lacked organization, apparently because of the newness of their teacher assistance program, the level of priority it was given by the district and district coordinator, and inaccessibility of or lack of importance placed on mentor training.

Washington Teacher Assistance Program surveys of participants show that the number of teachers being given the opportunity to participate in various elements of the program has steadily increased and that the program is having a progressively greater impact. TAP assessments also show that summer workshops for mentors significantly increase mentor effectiveness, serving both as an improvement tool and a networking tool, and efforts are being made to increase participation in this program statewide. Washington districts focusing on new teacher assistance program improvement report that they see a positive impact on their new teachers and on student learning.[15]

NOTES

1. Suzzane E. Wilson, Linda Darling-Hammond, and B. Berry, "Connecticut's Story: A Model of State Teaching Policy," Teaching Quality Policy Brief #4 (Seattle, WA: Center for the Study of Teaching and Policy, 2001).

2. Connecticut State Department of Education, Web Site for the Division of Evaluation and Research, 2002 (http://www.csde.state.ct.us/public/der/t-a/#best).

3. Thomas Sergei, Commissioner of Education, Connecticut State Department of Education, open letter to state school superintendents, 15 August 2002 (available at http://www.csde.state.ct.us/public/der/t-a/best/monographs/c5letter_best_update02.pdf).

4. To access the online seminars, type the following URL into your Web browser window: http://www.csde.state.ct.us/public/der/t-a/best/seminarseries/online_seminars/music/toc.htm.

5. Consortium of National Arts Education Associations, *National Standards for Arts Education* (Reston, VA: MENC, 1994).

6. National Assessment Governing Board (NAEP), *NAEP 1997 Arts Education Assessment Framework* (Washington, DC: Council of Chief State School Officers, 1994).

7. Barry Sweeney, "Best Practice Resources," 2002. Available for download at http://www.teachermentors.com/.

8. Connecticut State Department of Education, 2–3.

9. Ibid., 3.

10. Personal communication, interview transcripts, 16 August–21 November 2002.

11. Superintendent of Public Instruction, Washington State SPI, "Professional Education Guidelines, Teacher Assistance Program," 2003. Available online at http://www.k12.wa.us/cert/tap.

12. Ibid.

13. Superintendent of Public Instruction, Washington State SPI, *The Teacher Assistance Program: Report to the Legislature* (Olympia, WA: Author, 2001).

14. Ibid.

15. Ibid.

Mitchell Robinson is assistant professor of music education at Michigan State University.
Patti J. Krueger is professor and chair of music education in the School of Music at the University of Puget Sound.

Designing an Induction Program

Colleen M. Conway

Recent reports on induction at the national level identify thirty-eight states that offer some kind of program specifically targeted at novice teachers.[1] Although we should be encouraged that national policy makers are focusing on the important area of beginning teacher induction, if the provided programs are not perceived by music teachers to be valuable, then they are a waste of time and money.

Research has also suggested that there is great variation among policies for beginning teacher induction, much of it related to funding. Conway, Krueger, Robinson, Haack, and Smith suggest, "The practice of states dictating unfunded mandates for local districts to implement without accompanying increases in revenues, a long time public education policy ploy, appears to be alive and well in the new teacher induction arena."[2] For the most part, wealthier suburban districts often have detailed induction programs, while other types of districts do not. That the highest turnover rate of music teachers is in the urban and small rural programs is a problem for the profession.

As documented in the previous chapters and verified by the personal experience of most practitioners, even school districts that do provide induction programs rarely have the resources to provide a content-based induction program for music teachers. The first step in supporting music teachers through induction is to recognize the inability of many school districts to provide proper support. Music educators must become more active in the policy arena so that music teachers may receive professional development credit (also called in-service credit) for participating in induction programs that can be provided at the state, school district, and music department level. In Michigan, for example, beginning teachers must attend fifteen days of in-service training in the first three years of teaching (considered the "induction phase"). These in-service days are supposed to focus on content that is specific to beginning teachers.

State music organizations and members of the music industry have begun to offer programs targeted at the beginning music teacher. However, not all school districts will allow participation in these activities to "count" for the beginning music teacher. Some schools will allow only school district-sponsored professional development experiences to "count." Thus, the first step is for music educators to get involved in policy decision making. Administrators need to be educated about the value of content-specific professional development experiences for new music teachers. The second step is for state-, local-, and department-level music organizations to provide programs for beginning music teachers to meet the content-specific induction needs that cannot be met through generic programs. (For a list of ideas for designing a program, see the Suggestions for Organizing a State Music Organization or District Music Department Induction Program sidebar.)

TYPES OF WORKSHOPS AND GATHERINGS

Several years ago when I started studying beginning music teachers, fifteen first-year teachers came to our home for dinner during the third month of school. I distinctly remember saying to my husband as we were waiting for them to arrive, "Do you think I should try to facilitate discussion in some way?" I had written a list of questions for the teachers to ponder and discussion guides for me to use to learn about their experiences. Before my husband had a chance to answer the teachers began to arrive. About forty minutes later my husband caught me in the hallway and said, "Hey, let's tell these kids to keep an eye on Sarah (my then two-year-old) and let's you and I go to a movie." These teachers did not need any formal discussion guide. What they needed was time to just talk with one another about their experiences. As I reviewed audio and videotapes from this and other teacher gatherings, I was always struck by the depth of the new teacher conversations.

SUGGESTIONS FOR ORGANIZING A STATE MUSIC ORGANIZATION OR DISTRICT MUSIC DEPARTMENT INDUCTION PROGRAM

- Assign an officer or administrator for "Beginning Music Teacher Induction Support." This person is the "program chair" for events for beginning teachers.
- Assign another officer or administrator for "Beginning Music Teacher Mentor Support." (See Part III of this book for more details on mentoring programs.)
- Plan a summer workshop that provides activities for beginning teachers only (for both those who already have a job and others who are still looking).
- Provide evening and Saturday workshops at various sites during the school year. Move these workshops around the state (or the district) so teachers in all areas can get to them.
- Sponsor beginning teacher gatherings at all music association (or music department) events (i.e., during solo and ensemble days or All-County Band).
- Allow beginning teachers to substitute attendance at new teacher gatherings for required music association (or music department) work. For example, in Michigan all music teachers must work at solo and ensemble festivals. Excuse beginning teachers from these kinds of responsibilities.
- Invite members of the music industry to offer financial support for these events.

I have found that many beginning music teacher induction workshops are set up like mini-music education conferences. Several experienced teachers are brought in to tell beginning teachers how to be good teachers. This "stand and deliver" model is not what beginning teachers need. They need to interact. They need to talk and share their experiences with other beginners and with experienced teachers who may be able to offer assistance and suggestions. (For a list of possible topics for discussion, see the Suggested Topics for Workshops and Gatherings sidebar.)

CLASSROOM MANAGEMENT

All beginning teachers struggle with issues of classroom management. Although most district-sponsored programs attempt to focus on classroom management, music teachers teach in such diverse types of classrooms, and instruction is often so different from traditional classroom instruction, that music teachers are not enlightened by generic classroom management discussions. Induction workshops need to provide a place where teachers can describe their situations and experienced teachers and others can provide suggestions and assistance. I have often found it difficult to discuss classroom management outside of the specific classroom context. Without seeing for myself what the teacher is doing and how students are reacting, it is often hard to diagnose problems and offer suggestions. Induction program designers may consider a classroom management focus that includes a follow-up observation as a way to address this issue.

> **SUGGESTED TOPICS FOR WORKSHOPS AND GATHERINGS**
>
> - classroom management
> - parent interactions
> - administrative duties
> - choosing literature for performing groups
> - designing classroom activities for general music
> - standards-based planning
> - assessment of student learning

PARENT INTERACTIONS

Music teachers often deal with parents in different ways than do classroom teachers. In addition to communicating about travel, student grades, and student participation, they often interact with parents about the more thorny issues of roles in musicals, solos, and chair placement. In addition, they often have extended relationships with parents, since students are in music classes with the same music teacher for multiple years. Music teachers need advice from other music teachers about interacting with parents. Once again, programs should provide opportunities for beginning teachers to describe their situations and come up with solutions.

ADMINISTRATIVE DUTIES

Beginning music teachers (particularly at the secondary level) need guidance in regard to administrative duties. These include dealing with state organization fees, equipment and music budgets, solo and ensemble paper-work, festival paperwork, bus requests, parent meetings—the list goes on and on. A beginning music teacher induction program designed by a state music organization might include suggestions for organizing a music library, keeping track of inventory, and other administrative tasks. These are skills that are often specific to the teaching context. Thus, even if the beginning teacher has had sufficient preparation in a preservice program, there are still areas of music program administration that will be challenging for the beginning teacher.

CHOOSING LITERATURE AND CLASSROOM ACTIVITIES

The general teacher education literature suggests that lesson planning is one of the primary areas of concern for beginning teachers.[3] The specific concerns of music teachers include choosing literature for performing groups and design-ing classroom activities for general music classrooms of varying grade levels. A general education program will not provide the beginning music teacher with help in the areas most needed. Music induction programs should provide oppor-tunities and resources for beginning teachers to learn how to choose literature and design activities. Merely suggesting, "This is a good piece for festival," does not provide the teacher with the tools to make decisions about literature. Although most beginning teachers will have studied these topics in preservice programs, they need to review strategies now that they have a specific teaching context to plan for.

STANDARDS-BASED PLANNING AND ASSESSMENT

As previously mentioned, most preservice teachers will have been required to write lesson plans and rehearsal designs for standards-based instruction. However, I have found that most beginning teachers do not rely on the type of planning taught in their preservice classes when they begin to teach. In the words of a first-year teacher: "I have to deal with what is staring me in the face—the parent calls, the bus request, the instrument repair. I feel bad about it, but I basically grab my score and learn it along with the kids." I remember thinking "Ouch!" when I heard that quote in the interview. However, I do believe it reflects the experience of most beginning teachers. Many of these teachers did not attend K–12 music programs that were standards-based. Many of them student-taught in situations where their co-op teachers did not provide standards-based instruction. Although they have had experience with standards-based instruction and assess-ment techniques in college and university methods courses (an inauthentic expe-rience no matter what you do!), without assistance in the induction phase, it will be difficult for the beginning teacher to provide standards-based instruction and assessment. It is difficult to teach what you have never seen modeled.

OBSERVING EXPERIENCED MUSIC TEACHERS

Many beginning teachers have reported to me that watching experienced teachers has been a useful experience in the beginning years. One said: "It's so weird, we had to do all those observations of teachers during our undergraduate days and I never really felt like I was learning anything. Now that I have tried to be a teacher for a few months I wish I could go back and do all those observations again. Now I know what I'm looking at." I know that many states are trying to find ways to use retired teachers in the beginning teacher support process. One suggestion might be to find a way for the retired teachers to substitute so the beginning teachers can get out to observe.

> **SUGGESTED INDUCTION ACTIVITIES**
>
> • observing experienced music teachers
> • observing other novice teachers
> • receiving observations or clinics from music content specialists

OBSERVING OTHER NOVICE TEACHERS

Beginning teachers have also reported that observing their slightly older colleagues (second-, third-, and fourth-year teachers) has been a valuable induction activity. "When I went to see him [third-year teacher] I could sort of picture myself pulling off what he was doing. Sometimes when I watch a real experienced teacher I just feel like I'll never be that good," said one first-year teacher.

RECEIVING OBSERVATIONS OR CLINICS FROM MUSIC CONTENT SPECIALISTS

The general teacher education literature suggests that successful induction programs usually include the opportunity for beginning teachers to team-teach with experienced teachers in some format. Although this is difficult logistically for music teachers and school districts, it is the key to providing music teachers with experiences that go beyond mere discussion of good teaching to really improving music teaching and learning. Beginning teachers have reported that if regular team-teaching is not possible, even the occasional observation or clinic from an experienced teacher has been useful. In Michigan, the Michigan School Vocal Music Association (MSVMA) funds a "clinic" program. The beginning teacher contacts the MSVMA office, and the organization pays and makes arrangements for an experienced teacher to visit the classroom of the beginning teacher. (See the Suggested Induction Activities sidebar for a summary of appropriate activities.)

HONORING AND VALUING THE IDEAS OF BEGINNING TEACHERS

As any emerging professional, beginning teachers want to feel that they are making professional contributions. It is important for the music education profession to honor and value the perspective of the beginning teacher. As I mentioned previously, I have had many experienced teachers question the need for induction support by suggesting that "these teachers should not feel this way. They should not feel isolated or they should not feel overwhelmed." Ultimately, it does not matter what the experienced teachers think a beginning teacher should feel. Beginning teachers do feel isolated and they do have concerns. If we as a profession wish to retain beginning music teachers and shape them into the best music teachers they can be, then we must listen to their concerns. I see beginning music teachers as the future of the profession. Although there are some wonderful music programs throughout the country, there are a lot of areas for improvement in the profession, and new blood entering the system is the key to improvement.

NOTES

1. Recruiting New Teachers, Inc., *Learning the Ropes: Urban Teacher Induction Programs and Practices in the United States* (Belmont, MA: Author, 1999).

2. Colleen M. Conway, Patti J. Krueger, Mitchell Robinson, Paul Haack, and Michael V. Smith, "Beginning Music Teacher Induction and Mentor Policies: A Cross-state Perspective," *Arts Education Policy Review* 104, no. 2, (2002): 10.

3. Sharon Feiman-Nemser, Sharon Schwille, Cindy Carver, and Brian Yusko, *A Conceptual Review of Literature on New Teacher Induction* (E. Lansing, MI: National Partnership of Excellence and Accountability in Teaching [NPEAT], 1999), Document #Ed449147, Sponsored by the Office of Educational Research and Improvement, Washington, DC; Gary A. Griffin, ed., *The Education of Teachers. Ninety-Eighth Yearbook of the National Society for the Study of Education* (Chicago: University of Chicago Press, 1999); Leslie Huling-Austin, *Assisting the Beginner Teacher* (Reston, VA: Association of Teacher Educators, 1990); Leslie Huling-Austin, "Research on Learning to Teach: Implications for Teacher Induction and Mentoring Programs," *Journal of Teacher Education* 43, no. 3 (1992): 163–72; Leslie Huling-Austin, *Becoming a Teacher: What Research Tells Us* (Indianapolis, IN: Kappa Delta Pi Publications, 1994).

Colleen M. Conway is assistant professor of music education at the University of Michigan School of Music.

Induction Ideas for Music Teachers

Colleen M. Conway

We can all think of geographic areas of the country or types of music teacher positions for which providing appropriate induction experiences is logistically problematic. If there are no other music teachers in a school district or if there are no other schools or music programs for many miles, appropriate induction for the music teacher is a challenge. However, beyond advocating for more inclusive state-level policy and music organization induction programs, what can fellow music educators do?

As mentioned in the previous chapter, new music teachers need to have conversations with other music teachers about music teaching and learning. These conversations can be informal. In fact, in my recent inquiry into professional development experiences that are most meaningful to teachers throughout their careers, informal interactions with other teachers at conferences and meetings was listed as the primary source of professional development for experienced teachers.

Below are some suggestions for music teachers who want to help beginning teachers. I am suggesting that these are induction ideas rather than mentoring ideas because I believe that the concept of mentoring suggests multiple interactions, while informal induction may refer to a minimal time commitment (due to logistics) for both the new music teacher and the music teacher who is trying to help.

- Go out of your way to introduce yourself to the new teacher at music events. Even better, call the new music teacher at the beginning of the year and get to know him or her before music department or association events.
- Ask for details when you say, "How are things?" It usually won't take more than a few sentences from the beginning teacher before you get a sense of how you can help.

- Every time you do some administrative task of your job (filling out solo and ensemble registration forms or reserving the auditorium for the spring concert) call a beginning teacher (or two!) to remind him or her to do the same.
- Invite a beginning teacher to go to a local music store with you to choose literature for students (solos, method books, and small and large ensembles).
- Volunteer to teach for a day in the classroom of the beginning teacher so he or she can watch his or her students with an experienced teacher.
- Invite the beginning teacher to visit your school and give him or her the opportunity to work with your students as well.
- Every time you write a letter to parents (or cut and paste one from last year), e-mail a copy of the letter to a beginning teacher (or two) as a way to help him or her with the administrative work of the job.
- If you hear something nice about the beginning teacher (from a student, administrator, parent, or colleague), tell him or her about it!
- Listen to beginning teachers more than you give advice. Remember that they have been sitting in university courses for four or five years getting advice on being a teacher. They need to figure some things out for themselves.
- Ask the beginning music teacher about ideas he or she has about music teaching and learning. Beginning teachers want to feel that they have something to offer.

THE ROLE OF THE UNIVERSITY IN INDUCTION

Several states are exploring the idea that university faculty should be key players in the mentoring and induction process. Universities in Michigan, for example, are being asked by the state to document their interactions with and support of teacher education graduates. Universities in Ohio are held accountable for their graduates' performance on the Praxis II and Praxis III licensure tests. Praxis III is not taken until the second year of teaching has been completed. The well-funded beginning teacher programs in Connecticut and California require higher education participation. However, several issues present challenges to the involvement of higher education in the mentoring and induction process. Funding is inevitably a major issue in states that do not provide monies earmarked for induction. Universities rarely have the resources to follow their graduates into the field with induction and mentoring programs. In addition, if university professors are to help in the field, these responsibilities must become part of their regular teaching load, which presents yet another financial barrier. The ability to maintain continuity into the field (with the mobility of new teachers as well as university professors) may be an additional stumbling block in the development of induction programs that include university personnel.

Logistics aside, I have found that even informal induction interactions between university faculty and beginning music teachers are perceived by beginning music teachers as useful. I encourage university faculty to make every effort to provide these experiences. I feel that my interactions with beginning teachers in the study of induction and mentoring have improved my teaching practice as a university methods instructor and supervisor of student teachers, and my understanding of the world of the beginning music teacher has become clearer. I encourage others in university settings to also explore becoming involved in induction and mentoring.

Colleen M. Conway is assistant professor of music education at the University of Michigan School of Music.

PART III:
MENTORING

School District-Sponsored Mentor Programs

Colleen M. Conway

This chapter discusses the school district-sponsored mentor program experiences of thirteen beginning music teachers teaching in a variety of music settings (general, choral, and instrumental) in Michigan.[1] Profiles of each teacher with school and teaching schedule are provided in Figure 1.

LACK OF CONSISTENCY ACROSS SCHOOL DISTRICTS

The state of Michigan requires that all school districts provide mentors for beginning teachers: "Section 1526. For the first 3 years of his or her employment in classroom teaching, a teacher shall be assigned by the school in which he or she teaches to 1 or more master teachers, or college professors or retired master teachers, who shall act as mentor or mentors to the teacher."[2] However, there was no consistency in the interpretation of the Michigan law represented in this data. The teacher profiles in Figure 1 represent a vast spectrum of mentoring practices including teachers who were provided nonmusic mentors from out of the district (Tom and Marie), teachers who were provided nonmusic mentors from the district (Adam, James, Brian, and Joan), teachers who were provided with music mentors from the district (Trish, Allison, Mark, Elle, Teri, and Doug), and a teacher who was provided a music mentor from outside the district (Penny). The profiles are also inconsistent in the pay and training that the mentors received.

TYPE OF SCHOOL

There appears to be a connection between the size and type of school and the level of commitment on the part of the district to train and pay the mentors. In the four large suburban districts, all mentors were paid and trained. In the seven rural districts, mentors were paid and trained in three of the districts. In the two urban districts, the mentors were not paid or trained. Several mentors

FIGURE 1. TEACHER PROFILES

Participant	Type of School *	Teaching Responsibilities	Who Is Mentor?	Paid?	Trained?
Trish	Large/urban	6th-, 7th-, 8th-grade band	Vocal music teacher	No	No
Allison	Large/urban	K–3 general music (2 buildings)	HS band teacher (had been her student teaching co-op)	No	No
Elle	Large/suburban	5th- to 8th-grade strings	HS string teacher	Yes	Yes
Teri	Large/suburban	6th- to 8th-grade band	Band teacher (Grades 6–8) in another building in the district	Yes	Yes
Tom	Large/suburban	6th- to 8th-grade band	Band teacher (Grades 6–8) in another building in the district	Yes	Yes
Marie	Large/suburban	K–3 general music (2 buildings)	Retired classroom teacher working in county program	Yes	Yes
Mark	Medium/rural	Beginning elementary band, 6th-grade band, asst. HS band, asst. HS marching band, jazz band	Band teacher (team situation)	No	No
Doug	Medium/rural	5th- to 12th-grade band	HS choral teacher	Yes	Yes
Adam	Small/rural	5th- to 12th-grade band	Middle school English teacher	No	No
Brian	Small/rural	Beginning elementary band, 6th-grade band, 7th/8th-grade band, HS marching band	HS math teacher	Yes	Yes
Penny	Small/rural	5th- to 12th-grade band	Band teacher in nearby district	No	No
James	Small/rural	Beginning elementary band, 6th-grade band, 7th/8th-grade band, HS chorus, HS band, HS marching band	HS math teacher/former football coach	No	No
Joan	Small/rural	HS chorus; K–5 general music	Elementary librarian	Yes	Yes

* Large = 3,600 students or more K–12; medium = 1,200–3,600 students; small = 1,200 or fewer students.

This figure first appeared in Colleen M. Conway "An Examination of District-Sponsored Beginning Music Teacher Mentor Practices," Journal of Research in Music Education 51, no.1 (2003): 8. Reprinted with permission.

and principals commented on this issue. "Our district just does not have the resources like the suburban schools do to provide training or pay for mentors," said a rural school mentor. "This district has a very strong teachers union. Teachers are provided with many excellent programs," commented a suburban school principal. An urban school mentor said, "We have so many things to fix out here that the mentor program is just not a priority." That schools with more money are able to provide more for new teachers is not surprising. However, it is something the profession needs to reflect on. In Michigan, the state music organizations are beginning to look for ways to support new teachers in urban and rural schools who are not given appropriate mentor and induction experiences through the district.

TEACHING RESPONSIBILITIES AND CLASSROOM SETTING

Much of the research literature on beginning teachers suggests that a specific challenge for new teachers is that they are often assigned more difficult teaching loads and more difficult classes than experienced music teachers.[3] The data from the teacher profiles in Figure 1 suggests that the very nature of being a music teacher includes planning for multiple grade levels and possibly very diverse content areas. Joan sees children from ten different grade levels each week; Mark, Doug, Adam, Brian, Penny, and James see children from eight different grade levels; Marie from six; Allison, Elle, and Tom from four; and Trish and Teri from three.

Four of the teachers stay in one school building all day. Eight of the teachers are in two buildings each day, and one is in three different school buildings each day. Of the three teachers working in elementary music, Marie travels from classroom to classroom with a cart, Allison travels with a cart for some classes and is on the stage in the cafetorium for others, and Joan teaches on the floor in the cafeteria. These settings are not ideal for instruction.

For the ten teachers working in secondary music, responsibilities beyond classroom teaching include football games, parades, basketball games, women's sports events (in some cases), solo and ensemble festivals at junior high and high schools, band and orchestra festivals at junior high and high schools, musicals, graduation ceremonies, and many other community events. All of the secondary teachers travel somewhere with their ensembles as part of a short field trip or extended band, orchestra, or choir tour. These are tremendous responsibilities for any teacher, but particularly for a beginning teacher.

Michigan certifies music teachers to teach music in grades K–12. What this means is that many of these beginning teachers are teaching outside of their prepared content area (i.e., band, orchestra, or choir). James and Brian were teaching high school choral music, although neither had ever sung in a choir before accepting his teaching position. Brian was also teaching sixth-grade

71

general music, which is not an area he had been prepared to teach in pre-service education.

These findings are consistent with past studies[4] that suggest that some of the issues faced by beginning music teachers are music-specific and may be different from issues faced by the general classroom teacher. It is important for the music education profession to educate mentors and administrators about the inherently problematic teaching schedule and classroom context issues faced by music teachers.

ASSIGNMENT OF MENTORS

These profiles suggest that many administrators had tried to secure appropriate mentors for music teachers. All of the beginning teachers were provided with an experienced mentor. Seven of them were provided with music teacher mentors. Of the six who did not have music mentors, James was assigned to a mentor who was married to a music teacher. However, the criteria for choosing mentors varied greatly. Penny's principal said, "We have had a big turnover with music teachers in the program. We really want to support Penny so she will stay. However, she is the only instrumental music teacher in the district. Who can we provide her with? We decided to allow her to choose a mentor from outside the district so that she could have someone who would be useful for her." In Allison's case, her principal had initially assigned her to the building custodian. Although Allison worked to change this assignment so that she could have the high school band director in her district as her mentor, her principal thought his initial choice was logical. "I wanted to provide Allison with someone who knew the building but also understood music. Our building custodian plays drum set in a band so I thought he could be a real help to Allison," her principal said.

PAID AND TRAINED

Seven of the mentors had received formal training and guidelines for the mentoring process. However, all of the mentors suggested that training would be valued. "I would have liked to have had some more guidance regarding my role," said one mentor. "It was not really clear what the expectations of the mentor program were. Some sort of training may have helped that," commented another. Mentors and mentees in settings that provided no training were concerned that the expectations of the program were not clear. "I'm not really sure what he was supposed to help me with," said a first-year teacher. "We really did not know what we were supposed to do," a mentor said. The same seven mentors who were trained for the mentor program were also paid for their services. Several of the other mentors were unaware that mentors were paid in other districts. One of them said, "I guess I should ask about that. I never realized mentors were paid in other districts."

The Michigan state education department is currently developing more formalized "Standards for Beginning Teacher Induction and Mentor Programs."[5] The data from this study suggest that there is a strong need for state and local policy in these thirteen districts to assist the districts and administrators in the consistent design, implementation, and evaluation of beginning teacher mentoring programs. Several of the administrators interviewed in the study discussed the lack of funding and the vague requirements of the program. "The state just came down from above and told us 'you will have a mentor program.' But without money to support it we just cannot provide what the state is asking," said one principal. "It has never really been clear to me what the state requirements are regarding mentoring," commented another principal. Conway, Krueger, Robinson, Haack, and Smith provide a national policy overview and a comprehensive discussion of the policy issues associated with beginning music teacher induction and mentoring.[6]

TEACHER PERCEPTIONS OF VALUE

There was variation in the degree and type of contact between mentors and mentees. Figure 2 represents the degree and type of contact the thirteen teachers experienced. It also shows the mentees' perceptions of the value of the mentoring relationship.

The degree of contact between mentors and mentees appears to be related to the requirements of the mentoring program (for Brian, Joan, and Teri), the proximity of the mentor (for Trish, Doug, Elle, and Mark), or the existence of a previously established relationship (for Allison). Brian, Joan, and Teri were required to meet regularly with their mentors. The mentors were paid for the meetings, and all the meetings took place. Trish and her mentor were on the same teaching team, and the team met each Friday for lunch. Doug and his mentor taught in neighboring rooms at the high school every morning. Elle and Mark were in team-teaching situations. Allison had a previously established relationship with her mentor, so they also met regularly. Overall, when the school district-sponsored program required interaction, teachers met. When teachers were teaching in classrooms close to one another, they were more apt to meet. Although Allison's district did not require meetings and she and her mentor were not in the same school building, Allison and her mentor had a previously established relationship, which led to more frequent interactions.

All the teachers who had music mentors suggested that their mentoring relationships were somewhat valuable or valuable. In Trish's case, because her mentor was a vocal teacher instead of an instrumental teacher, the relationship was perceived as only somewhat valuable. Allison had a previously established relationship with her mentor and suggested, "My mentor really saved me this year. I don't know what I would have done without him." Although Elle and her

FIGURE 2. DEGREES OF CONTACT BETWEEN BEGINNING TEACHERS AND MENTORS

Participant	Degree of Contact	Type of Contact	Perceived Relationship as Valuable
Trish	Weekly fine arts team meetings	Lunch conversations	Somewhat
Allison	Weekly meetings and e-mail	After school/weekend meetings, dinners, conversations	Yes
Elle	Every day (team teachers)	Informal discussions, some lunches/dinners	Somewhat
Teri	E-mail several times per week Meetings about twice per month	E-mail, after-school meetings	Yes
Tom	No real contact	Mentor observed a few times with no real interaction	No
Marie	No real contact	Mentor observed a few times with no real interaction	No
Mark	Every day (team teachers)	Informal discussions, some lunches/dinners	Yes
Doug	Every morning at HS together	Information conversations	Somewhat
Adam	A few informal conversations	Hallway conversations, one observation	Somewhat
Brian	Required to meet 30 times	After-school meetings	Somewhat
Penny	A few conversations	Phone conversations, one observation	Somewhat
James	A few informal conversations	Hall conversations, 1–2 evening phone calls	Somewhat
Joan	Weekly meetings	Lunches together, informal conversations	Yes

This figure first appeared in Colleen M. Conway "An Examination of District-Sponsored Beginning Music Teacher Mentor Practices," Journal of Research in Music Education 51, no.1 (2003): 14. Reprinted with permission.

mentor were team teachers, she sometimes wished that she could have had a mentor outside of the music department: "I really would have liked to get to know some other teachers. My mentor was really great, but I think I would have liked to have gotten to know someone else. We were going to get to know one another anyway." Teri's mentor had the same position as she did in another middle school in the district. He was a veteran teacher and was able to provide her with a great deal of support: "I consider these two my 'model mentor team'" (researcher's log).

In his examination of the interactions of four music mentor-mentee pairs in Oregon, Montague suggested that the mentor-mentee relationship is a complex situational context.[7] Due to the situational nature of the mentoring relationship, it may be difficult to make concrete suggestions for creating a successful mentoring relationship. Every mentor-mentee pair is different. However, the study described in this chapter suggests that there must be some sort of interaction between the mentor and the mentee. Pairs who were required to meet met more often. In addition, music mentors were perceived by beginning music teachers as more valuable than nonmusic mentors.

CONTENT OF BEGINNING MUSIC TEACHER AND MENTOR INTERACTIONS

Administrative Duties

The most common theme in the discussions between mentors and beginning teachers was administrative issues. The beginning teachers working with secondary ensembles (particularly marching band) suggested that this area was the greatest challenge they faced in their new position. Mark said, "I spend most of my time on the administrative stuff associated with my job. I asked my mentor a lot of questions about all of that." Penny's principal commented, "We give our band director a one-period released time to deal with the administrative duties. There are so many things that she must keep track of."

Budgets, fund-raising, tours, weekend events, and other duties take sophisticated skill in time management and administrative organization. All of the beginning teachers suggested that they were unprepared for these tasks. A successful mentor for a beginning music teacher must be able to provide support in this area.

Classroom Management

The literature on beginning teachers in general education cites classroom management as a key area of concern for beginning teachers. Music teachers also asked many questions in this content area. "I asked my mentor to help me with what to do with discipline. She did not always know what to tell me, but it was good to talk about it," said Brian. "We talked a lot about discipline and management. It seems like this is an even bigger issue in music classes because the classes are often very large and the students are holding noise-makers," Brian's mentor commented. Doug's principal said, "I know he needed a lot of help with management. All of our new teachers do. I was glad to be able to provide an experienced mentor to help him with the issues of large classes."

This suggests that it is important for a mentor to be available to observe in the classroom of the mentee. In order for useful classroom management discussions to be a part of the relationship, mentors and mentees must understand the mentee's classroom context.

Parent Interactions

Many of the beginning teachers talked to their mentors about issues concerning interactions with parents. This theme may be more prevalent among beginning music teachers since they generally see many more students per week than a typical classroom teacher. "I had quite a few problems with parents in the beginning of the year. The Booster Group just had some real outspoken parents. My mentor gave me some good advice regarding dealing with those parents," said Penny. "Dealing with the parent group was one of the hardest things in the beginning. My mentor helped me a lot with suggestions for how to approach parents," James commented.

Building and District Policies

Many of the mentors' questions concerned building and district policies. Those beginning teachers who did not have assigned mentors in their buildings said that they found someone else (often a secretary) in the building to assist them with their many questions. "I tried to make sure to keep my new teacher updated on all the things going on in the building. He seemed to have a lot of questions about assemblies and conference days and things like that," said Brian's mentor. Penny said, "The secretaries really knew me. I felt pretty stupid, but I just went to them for everything. How do I do this? When do I do that?" Mark's principal said, "I think it is quite important for a new teacher to have an assigned mentor in the building. Someone needs to help them get settled with building issues."

Although this issue is faced by all beginning teachers, when you consider that the majority of the thirteen teachers in the study were in at least two buildings per week, this issue becomes even more problematic.

Personal Issues

In some cases, beginning teachers talked to their mentors about personal issues that were not directly related to school. "It was good for me to have someone to talk to about my car troubles, my rent, stuff like that," Allison said. "We really became friends. We spent a good portion of our mentor time just talking about other non-school related things," said Trish. Although all beginning teachers discuss isolation as a beginning teacher concern, the fact that these music teachers were usually the only music teacher in the building and often the only music teacher in the district makes having someone else to talk to a very important beginning music teacher issue.

The content of mentoring interactions documented in this study is consistent with areas of concern for beginning music teachers documented in previous music education literature.[8] However, the next section regarding curricular questions has not been previously addressed.

Curricular Questions

Very few of the beginning teachers said that they spoke to mentors about curricular issues. As I began to analyze my data and saw that curricular questions were not a part of the mentor-mentee interactions, I asked several of the beginning teachers specifically about this issue in follow-up interviews. The beginning teachers who did not have music mentors responded that they really could not talk to their mentors about music since their mentors did not know the subject. "She does not know anything about music, so it was not even something I thought about talking about," said Brian. The teachers who did have music mentors suggested that other issues such as administrative duties and classroom management seemed so much more pressing that they just never got around to reflecting on curricular issues. "I have to deal with what is staring me in the face right now. The bus requests, the fund-raising, the parent calls— they all need to be dealt with right now. As far as what I actually teach, I can survive if I pick up the score and go read it with the kids. It's all about survival right now," Penny said.

I am concerned that merely surviving during the first year of teaching will not encourage teachers to develop a reflective teaching practice that is so desperately needed in education. Beginning teachers need to be asking curricular questions and interacting with experienced music mentors in meaningful ways about instruction. However, the current configuration of beginning music teacher positions makes this growth nearly impossible. In one of the districts in the study, the instrumental music teacher was scheduled to teach only four periods in a five-period day because the district has recognized that the administrative duties of the position are so vast. This may be the kind of flexibility that is needed for beginning music teachers to have the time to develop. However, without a music mentor to encourage curricular dialogue, the beginning teacher cannot be expected to know what to ask.

Music Mentors for Music Teachers

It appears from this data that the beginning music teachers' level of satisfaction with the mentoring interactions was related to whether or not the mentor was a music teacher. All seven teachers who had music mentors felt that their mentoring interactions were at least somewhat valuable.

All participants suggested that music teachers need music mentors. For example, one principal said, "We just did not have anyone who was really appropriate as a mentor for him. There are no other music teachers. I guess we should consider something else though because I do think a music mentor would be good." Trish commented, "I am so glad that I had a music mentor. I don't think anyone else would really have understood what I am facing."

Even when nonmusic mentor relationships were perceived by teachers, mentors, principals, and myself as successful, participants suggested the need for music mentors. Brian's mentor said, "He and I really got along well. But there was not much I could do for him in terms of his teaching. I don't know anything about music." Several participants suggested that beginning music teachers need both music teacher mentors and building mentors. "I think music teachers need a music mentor and a building mentor. I guess I'm dreaming that that could happen," said Elle in focus group conversation. Teri's mentor said, "It was hard for me when I was not in the building. I think a building mentor would have helped her too." A principal commented, "As I'm talking with you, I'm beginning to think that maybe music teachers need two mentors."

SUGGESTIONS FOR MUSIC MENTOR PRACTICE BASED ON THE MICHIGAN EXPERIENCES

Assign a Mentor Early

In several instances, mentors were not assigned or identified until well into September. All of the participants suggested that it is in those first few days and weeks of school that beginning teachers need the most help. "It took a while before I knew who my mentor would be. This was kind of a problem because most of my questions were about the first day," said Joan. "I had some serious classroom management issues at band camp in the summer. Who was supposed to help me with that?" James asked.

Schedule So Mentors Can Observe

Many participants suggested that mentors need to be available to observe beginning teachers in their settings. "We really could not talk too much about my classroom because she was always teaching when I was and could never come and see me," Doug commented. "There really does need to be some way to work it out so the mentors can be available to observe the teachers while they are teaching. It is just really hard to schedule," said one principal. Brian's mentor said, "It would have been easier to talk about curricular things if I had been able to observe him teaching."

78

Several of the beginning teachers suggested that my presence in their classroom on the days I observed as part of data collection was valuable to their professional growth. "I wish my mentor could do more of what you did while you were here today," Marie said. Teachers believe that mentors serving in this classroom assistance role would be useful.

Opportunities for Getting to Know One Another

The teachers who had opportunities for getting to know one another outside of the mentoring relationship felt that these more social opportunities helped the relationship. "We had team meetings every Friday, so we got to know each other early on," said Trish. "We team-teach all day, so mentoring just sort of comes out of that," Mark's mentor said. Elle's principal commented, "They teach together all day long, so I think mentoring is just an outgrowth of what they do."

The teachers who had previously established relationships with their mentors suggested that this helped them to focus on important issues early on. Allison said, "We already knew each other from my student-teaching semester so we did not need to get to know each other." Several teachers suggested that the mentoring program in their district needed to include more opportunity for just getting to know one another. Adam said, "We needed to have some sort of beginning-of-the-year lunch or something so we could just get to know one another."

One of the criteria for mentoring programs should be that mentors and mentees have some informal opportunities to get to know one another. In addition, this type of meeting might help to establish clearer expectations about what the mentor and mentee relationship could be.

CONCLUSION

This examination of the thirteen district-sponsored mentor practices reveals a lack of consistency in the types of mentoring programs in the schools and varying degrees of teacher satisfaction with the programs. Variations in program offerings appear to be connected to the type of school, the teaching responsibility and classroom setting, the type of mentor assigned, and the degree to which that mentor was paid or trained. Teacher perceptions of the value of the program appear to be connected with the degree and type of contact with the assigned mentor. The content of mentoring interactions included administrative duties, classroom management, parent interaction, building and district policies, and personal issues. The need for music mentors is stressed due to the lack of interactions that focused on curricular issues. General suggestions for mentoring practices provided by the various participants (teachers, mentors, administrators, and the researcher) include early assignment of the mentor, scheduling so mentors can observe the beginning teachers, and opportunities for the mentor and mentee to get to know one another.

Although many of the issues that surfaced in this study go beyond the scope of providing for the beginning music teacher (i.e., lack of consistency in state-provided programs), music educators and music education researchers need to continue to work to have a voice in policy decisions and reform efforts that will affect the teaching and learning of music. University music teacher educators must work in conjunction with K–12 music educators and with state music organizations to advocate for appropriate mentoring programs for beginning music teachers. It may be that school districts cannot provide for the music-specific needs of the beginning music teacher. Programs designed and implemented by state music organizations may be the answer to providing content support. However, these programs should be designed based on research on beginning teachers and not just on the wisdom of leaders of state music organizations.

Music teacher education is often the brunt of attacks about poor teacher preparation. However, the problematic areas identified in this study (administrative duties, classroom management, parent interactions, and district policies) are areas that cannot be mastered until a beginning teacher arrives in a specific teaching context. Thus, the profession must work to provide support for music teachers once they are employed. Support for beginning teachers is not just a technique for addressing first-year survival and teacher retention. If beginning teachers are to be able to implement innovative teaching approaches learned in teacher preparation programs, they are going to need assistance in grappling with the messy issues in school change and curriculum reform.[9]

NOTES

1. More details regarding the methodology and research that supported these findings can be found in my article, "An Examination of District-Sponsored Beginning Music Teacher Mentor Practices," *Journal of Research in Music Education* 51, no. 1 (2003): 6–23.

2. Michigan Department of Education, *Guidelines and Recommendations for the New Teacher Induction/Teacher Mentoring Process in Michigan* (Lansing, MI: Author, 1994), 32.

3. Sharon Feiman-Nemser, "Teacher Mentoring: A Critical Review," *Eric Clearinghouse on Teaching and Teacher Education*, 1993 (http://www.ericsp.org/95-2/html); Yvonne Gold, "Beginning Teacher Support: Attrition, Mentoring and Induction," in *Handbook of Research on Teacher Education*, ed. J. Sikula, 2nd ed. (New York: Macmillan, 1996), 548–94; Sandra J. Odell and Douglas P. Ferraro, "Teacher Mentoring and Teacher Retention," *Journal of Teacher Education* 43, no. 4 (1992): 200–04.

4. Colleen M. Conway and Mandi Garlock, "The First Year of Teaching K–3 General Music: A Case Study of Mandi," *Contributions to Music Education* 29, no. 2 (2002): 9–28; Lisa DeLorenzo, "Perceived Problems of Beginning Music Teachers," *Bulletin of the Council for Research in Music Education,* no. 113 (1992): 9–25; Patti J. Krueger, "New Music Teachers Speak out on Mentoring," *Journal of Music Teacher Education* 8, no. 2 (1999): 7–13; Patti J. Krueger, "Reflections of Beginning Music Teachers," *Music Educators Journal* 88, no. 3 (2001): 51–54.

5. Michigan Department of Education, *Mentoring and Induction Standards* draft (Lansing, MI: Author, 2000).

6. Colleen M. Conway, Patti J. Krueger, Mitchell Robinson, Paul Haack, and Michael V. Smith, "Beginning Music Teacher Induction and Mentor Policies: A Cross-state Perspective," *Arts Education Policy Review* 104, no. 2, (2002): 9–18.

7. Matthew G. Montague, "Processes and Situatedness: A Collective Case Study of Selected Mentored Music Teachers" (Ph.D. diss., University of Oregon, 2000).

8. DeLorenzo, "Perceived Problems of Beginning Music Teachers"; Krueger, "New Music Teachers Speak out on Mentoring" and "Reflections of Beginning Music Teachers"; Montague, "Processes and Situatedness"; Michael V. Smith, "The Mentoring and Professional Development of New Music Educators: A Descriptive Study of a Pilot Program" (Ph.D. diss., University of Minnesota, 1994).

9. Conway et al., "Beginning Music Teacher Induction and Mentor Policies."

Colleen M. Conway is assistant professor of music education at the University of Michigan School of Music.

A Model Mentor Project

Michael V. Smith

   In response to growing calls for educational reform, a Task Force on Music Teacher Education was chartered in the fall of 1984 by the Society for Music Teacher Education of Music Educators National Conference (MENC). Recognizing that the professional practices of the 1990s would shape the course for music education well into the future, the group was charged with preparing a document that could direct and inform music teacher preparation in the twenty-first century. MENC and the Yamaha Corporation of America provided financial support.

   Initially, the committee was made up largely of Midwestern representation so that meetings could be conveniently arranged. However, as the need for broader MENC constituent input was felt, Yamaha provided support so that meetings could be held in several parts of the country (Chicago, Illinois; Tempe, Arizona; Austin, Texas; St. Paul, Minnesota; Wichita, Kansas; Reston, Virginia; and Anaheim, California).

   The final report dealt with identifying potential music educators, educating and training potential educators, and the mentoring and professional development of new music educators.

   Yamaha followed up its support of the committee by establishing a research program intended to experiment with the three phases through trial implementations. Several people on the original committee were given the responsibility to carry on development, trial, and evaluation of each particular aspect. Phase 1, Recruitment, Selection, and Retention: Choosing Music Educators for the Next Century, was the responsibility of A. Peter Costanza and his team at The Ohio State University. Phase 2, Teacher Certification Programs: The Process of Developing Music Educators, was assigned to Gerald Olson and the University of Wisconsin, Madison. Phase 3, Professional Development Programs: Planning for Career Growth, was carried out at the University of Minnesota under the

83

direction of Paul Haack. A parallel mentoring program directed by Steve Hedden was also undertaken for a year at the University of Arizona. These two latter programs, following the same general approach, provided a cross-check for geographic consistency. Results of the two programs were similar and contributed to the fine-tuning of the Minnesota program, which was carried into a second year of study.

EXPERIMENTAL FORMAT OF THE PROGRAM

The first year of the program began with facilitating mentoring relationships between fourteen first- or second-year music educators and seven experienced, successful mentor music teachers at each site. Specific references that follow are for the Minnesota program and, unless otherwise noted, were closely paralleled by the Arizona program.

Meeting formats took the shape of seven dinner meetings held from the second through the eighth month of the school year. These sessions began with a light dinner in a setting that encouraged participants to interact informally. This was followed by a more structured session based on the identified needs of the participants. (See Figure 1 for a needs survey.) The monthly group meetings usually concluded with time for individualized mentoring and planning of visits between mentors and mentees. General communication beyond and between these meetings was done through a newsletter. Articles in this publication included a review of the previous meeting's presentation, organizational matters, and additional professionally related articles, idea tips, and suggestions gathered from the mentors.

Between meetings, individualized mentoring was carried on by telephone calls and visits to one another's schools. Mentors were expected to spend one full day or two half-days at the mentee's school to become acquainted with the teaching situation, observe teaching, discuss instruction strategies, and otherwise work with the new teacher. In turn, each mentee was allowed a half-day visit to the mentor's school. These individualized discussions and visits, along with the group meetings, provided the general framework for the program.

Initially, area music coordinators were contacted to solicit their help in identifying appropriate candidates for participation in the program. These coordinators, along with an advisory group of school and university teachers, met to discuss possible meeting formats, programming approaches, visit exchange complications and procedures, identification of first- and second-year teachers in the metropolitan area, and identification of excellent teachers as potential mentors.

The potential mentees were contacted by letter and subsequently by telephone to discuss their participation. They were selected so that a variety of levels and emphases in music education, as well as a variety of districts, would be represented. Mentors were then contacted in a similar manner and were

FIGURE 1. PERSONAL NEEDS SURVEY FOR TEACHERS

Concern levels: Rate on a 1–10 scale, with 1 representing an area of great concern or discomfort.

____ Classroom (music room) management/discipline
____ Problem-solving skills
____ Communication skills
____ Interpersonal skills
____ General knowledge of music fundamentals, history, and literature
____ Knowledge of teaching methods
____ Conducting skills
____ Rehearsal skills
____ Arranging/composing skills
____ Keyboard skills
____ Improvisation skills
____ Ethnic/multicultural music education
____ Social/psychological uses and functions of music
____ Curriculum development/instructional design
____ Daily class planning and organization
____ Student evaluation and grading
____ Special learner accommodations
____ Applied learning theory
____ Understanding and using research
____ Computer skills
____ Skills with other educational/musical technology
____ Knowledge of administrative/political structures and procedures
____ Music program administration
____ Defending and advocating music in the curriculum

List any other areas you feel particularly comfortable about:

_____

List any other areas you feel particularly uncomfortable about:

_____

Note. This figure first appeared in Paul Haack and Michael V. Smith, "Mentoring New Music Teachers," Music Educators Journal 87, no. 3 (2000): 26. Reprinted with permission.

selected on the basis of their match with the levels and areas of instructional emphasis represented among the mentees.

Each mentor was paired with two mentees from different geographical regions of the metropolitan area, thus avoiding mentors and mentees from the same school district being paired. This was done to provide mentees with different perspectives than they might receive from their own district and to assure that the process would not be part of a formal district evaluation program.

INITIAL MEETINGS

The first meeting of the Project 2000 Mentoring Program was held in October of 1991. Fourteen mentees and seven mentors gathered at the University of Minnesota for dinner and a program. The focus of the initial program was primarily on the mentoring process and facilitating opportunities for the young teachers to learn from their experienced colleagues. We discovered from the outset, however, that the dialogues were not only between mentors and mentees, and not only during the formal meeting hours. Rather, discussions and conversations developed between mentees as well as between mentors, often well beyond the scheduled meeting times, and eventually extended to self-arranged breakfast or dinner meetings.

Subsequent meetings flowed comfortably within the same general format, beginning with the informal dinner and conversation time and concluding with the more structured program. Such a format seemed to allow good interactions between mentoring groups and allowed the teachers to catch up with one another in a pleasant, relaxed environment before moving to the more structured program for the evening. Final program evaluations from the study participants rated the effects of the comfortable conversations over food to be among the most valuable of the mentoring experiences. The positive impact of "breaking bread together" cannot be underestimated.

As noted earlier, along with these regular mentoring dinners, the project also supported released time so that mentors were able to visit mentees for a whole day or two half-days, in the mentee's own school setting. Allowing mentees a half-day of released time so that they might observe their mentors in the mentor's own school setting was also found helpful. Such mutual visits seemed to be very valuable in helping mentors offer realistic, concrete, and useful ideas and suggestions about practical situations and concerns the young teachers faced.

THE SECOND YEAR

In the second year, modifications were made based on the participants' experiences of the project in its first year and some new ideas that were introduced. A notable change was the creation of "mentoring triads." Peer mentoring was introduced in the model as some mentees from the first year continued in the program for the second year. "Triads," consisting of a mentor, a first-year mentee, and a second-year mentee, were formed to work together as mentoring teams. Second-year evaluations revealed that such a configuration allowed for a variety of insights from the varying perspectives that the different levels of professional experiences brought to each mentoring team. Both short-term and long-term professional development strategies were represented by the various levels of professional maturity within each mentoring group. First-year mentees, of course, received important initial professional guidance, but also brought with them new ideas and idealism that both challenged and refreshed older professionals. Second-year mentees also received continued support in their development, but their growing abilities were also affirmed as they were given opportunities to share with and guide the youngest teacher of the triad. After all, they were probably in the best position to understand the problems of a first-year teacher, having just been one. Finally, mentor teachers were given the opportunity to share professional wisdom and insights gathered over the course of establishing a respected career, but were also renewed in both practice and spirit by the ideas and methods of their younger counterparts.

Other insights into mentor-mentee pairing were gleaned from the first-year experience and modified in the second year. It was discovered, for example, that young junior high music instructors preferred to have mentors who also taught at the junior high school level. Mentors who instructed at the senior high level were not perceived as having the same understanding or facility with the methods and materials for this level as would a practitioner who worked with students of this age daily. In addition, it was determined that a two-to-one mentee-mentor ratio was most effective.

The schedules of the secondary mentors presented another challenge. Because of their demanding extracurricular calendars, they were not always capable of following through in as timely a manner as they wished with their mentoring responsibilities. Mentor candidates should from the outset be informed of the necessary time commitments, the effort required, and the importance of committing to such a relationship.

In addition to changing the way mentors and mentees were paired, the manner and style in which participants worked together were considered during the second year of the project. A "Mentoring Style Indicator" developed by William Gray and a "Mentoring Style Questionnaire" written by Elizabeth Alleman were both introduced in an effort to come to a better understanding of what mentoring methods appeared to be most effective for the participants.

The Gray Mentoring Style Indicator (MSI) helps reveal appropriate strategies for offering help to young professionals. Based on the premise that the mentoring relationship passes through stages as the younger professional moves from dependence to levels of growing independence, the MSI allows mentees and mentors to become more aware of the manner in which they are both most comfortable in receiving help, as well as the style in which each mentor is most comfortable offering assistance (see Figure 2). The MSI exercise suggested that all of the individuals in this particular mentoring project showed a preference for a collaborative mentoring style.

FIGURE 2. GRAY MENTORING STYLES

Prescriptive (M-p)*	Persuasive (Mp)	Collaborative (MP)	Confirmative (mP)
Mentor gives concrete directions grounded in realistic and tangible methodology.	Mentor allows for more protégé independence but still offers ideas, suggestions, and coaching.	Mentor emphasizes cooperation and joint decision making.	Protégé has become nearly self-sufficient but continues to look to mentor for confirmation and support.

*M=mentor; P=protégé

The Alleman Mentoring Style Questionnaire consists of a series of one hundred Likert-type items that are designed to measure the amount and quality of mentoring activities. Ten discrete behaviors determined to be central to mentoring are identified and measured by the survey. These behaviors are teaching the job, teaching politics, offering challenging tasks, counseling, offering career help, demonstrating trust, endorsing or affirming actions and/or views, sponsoring, protecting, and offering friendship. All ten items, especially counseling, trust, teaching the job, and giving political tips, were found to be important aspects of mentoring relationships for the participants in the project.

As with the first year of the project, programs for second-year meetings were directed by responses to a needs survey. Not surprisingly, many of the areas of concern mentioned by the new teachers in the first year of the project continued to be areas of interest for participants in the second year. As a result, some program areas from the first year were carried into the second. It was both interesting and encouraging to note that there did appear to be a difference between first- and second-year mentees in their comfort level concerning these issues. There was also a growing sense of the importance of the mentoring relationship's impact on their own professional growth. "Talking to some of the first-year mentees reinforced the fact that I had learned a lot in one year! It felt wonderful to be able to help someone else," said one second-year mentee.

CONCLUSION OF THE PROGRAM

The Project 2000 Mentoring Program concluded formally at the end of the 1992–93 school year. The Minnesota Music Educators Association took over portions of the program. A breakfast for new teachers continues to be hosted at the organization's annual conference (and also in Illinois with the Illinois Music Educators Association, as one of the coordinators for the program moved to that state). Some professional programs continue to be offered at state meetings as well. Pairing mentors and mentees continues, but in a limited and less comprehensive manner. There is, for example, no ongoing monitoring of mentoring pair activities, nor, without funding, is there any expectation that in-school mentor and mentee visits will occur.

SOME RESULTS AND CONCLUSIONS

Music educators often do their jobs in relative isolation. An important benefit of this experimental project was the collegiality and emotional support that participants experienced through their associations with one another. Both mentees and mentors expressed an appreciation for the opportunity to gather regularly in a non-evaluative, supportive environment to interact with other music teachers. Participants indicated that two program strategies seemed to be particularly helpful in promoting this supportive and helpful mentoring environment: the informal dinner portion of the monthly meetings, and providing the opportunity for mentors and mentees to visit one another in their own classroom situations. In addition, the creation of mentoring triads during the second year provided further opportunities for interaction with music education colleagues and peers.

Data collected from the study of the program indicated that participants felt it had provided valuable mentoring experiences and professional development opportunities. Beginning teachers mentioned that particular help was given in classroom management and discipline, knowledge of teaching materials, daily classroom planning, special learner accommodations, skill with music technology, and knowledge of political structures. As mentioned, all participants indicated a preference for a collaborative style of mentoring.

The organizers of Project 2000 sincerely hope that this study will be of assistance in the development of other mentoring and professional development programs for new music teachers, so that many others might experience the joy and satisfaction of being involved in the professional lives of others.

Michael V. Smith is associate professor and chair of music education at DePaul University in Chicago.

Breaking the Isolation:
Beginning Music Teacher Views on Collaboration
Patti J. Krueger

> I can't imagine what my first year would have been like if I hadn't had a mentor who was an experienced music teacher! Much of my success this year is due to my mentor's work with me. (First-year general music teacher, Interview 7, 2003)

> My advice to new teachers is to be ready to adapt to whatever situations they face, and find people to ask for help. Things are never what you think of as ideal, but with help, you can make an initially startling situation become positive. You have to realize that kids are talented in different ways, and you can bring out their best if you do a little evaluating and brainstorming with other teachers. I had situations that I didn't expect, and I learned how to deal with them positively without being disappointed. You have to create ways of providing students with the opportunities they should have, and you can rarely do this alone. (First-year high school choral music teacher, Interview 13, 1999)

New teachers require significant support in their first years of teaching to effectively implement all they need to know in their classrooms. The transition from student teaching in an experienced teacher's classroom to solo teaching in a first job is often a startling and challenging process. What do new music teachers say about finding themselves isolated from other teachers, about their mentors, and about the types and sources of support they see as being most effective? This chapter will examine these questions from the point of view of first-year music teachers.

In my own experience as a beginning music teacher in 1978, I found myself alone in my first music classroom with no other teachers in sight during the school day. Looking for a challenge, I had taken a job in a small northern Wisconsin town with a significant Native American population, far from my previous support systems. I soon realized that I needed to seek out some answers to my classroom problems, and I enrolled in weekend courses at a university several hours away. I began to search for an understanding of what was going on between clashing cultures in my own classroom, school, and community. The isolation of my first year of teaching led me to take a new public school teaching position the next year in an area closer to my university studies. This initial year of teaching had a lasting impact on my career path, eventually leading me to work with beginning teachers.

In contrast to my first teaching situation, research on new teacher development suggests that teachers learn best when they can build their own knowledge and curriculum, share ideas with colleagues, and practice what they have learned in their classrooms.[1] Other studies show that collaboration with peers and experienced teachers can foster intellectual growth and reflection in new teachers, allowing them to examine classroom problems and make changes in their practice.[2] A comment from one new music teacher illustrates this point:

> My mentor came to my classroom and observed me several times, and I observed her. She asked me questions about my teaching, and she shared her ideas and materials with me. In talking with her, I could figure out where my curriculum was going for the year, how to try new ideas with students, and what to do about things I was having trouble with. She was always willing to spend time with me whenever we met, and this was definitely my most important help all year. (First-year general music teacher, Interview 10, 2003)

With help from her mentor, this new music teacher describes learning to analyze her classroom work and her interactions with students, trying new approaches to classroom problems, and creating a curriculum for her classroom.

Despite these findings, a number of studies indicate that beginning teachers feel anxious and isolated during their transition into teaching, and often experience little significant collegial support during the first year.[3] Lortie emphasized isolation of beginning teachers from their colleagues as significantly influencing their problems and practice and as a major cause of attrition among new teachers.[4] These studies illustrate what can happen when new teachers work in isolation from each other and from their more experienced colleagues, without sufficient means for sharing daily problems, ideas, and practices.

In the field of music, research findings indicate that isolation from other music teachers and resource people is a significant problem for many beginning music teachers.[5] Beginning music teachers need to discuss their work, but they often do not have experienced people who have seen them teach and who are not a part of the formal evaluation process within their school. DeLorenzo found that, when present, experienced music teachers were perceived to provide the most significant mentoring support during the first year of teaching, and concluded that music teachers often need help with very music-specific concerns and problems.[6] What do new music teachers say about feeling isolated from other teachers during the first year of teaching, and how do they move beyond this problem to collaboration with other teachers? The quotes in this chapter giving voice to new teachers come from a study of beginning music teachers in Washington State,[7] as well as first-year music teachers in Washington interviewed for this chapter in 2003.

THE REALITIES OF NEW TEACHER ISOLATION

> I felt quite alone as a new general music teacher, especially after being a student for four years with peers all around. Luckily, I worked one day a week at a second school, and I could watch the end of another music teacher's classes if I arrived early. These brief, stolen moments were my main source of ideas and materials all year! I had very little contact with other music teachers this year. (First-year general music teacher, Interview 8, 1999)

A sense of isolation from other teachers is commonly voiced by many new music teachers. Many describe isolation from other music teachers in their area of expertise as being one of their primary struggles during the first year. Sometimes, working an extended day and being the only music teacher in their school or schools, these new teachers find it difficult to network or share common problems and ideas with others doing similar work. Some teachers find themselves removed from daily interaction with other teachers at their schools:

> I've made a real effort to talk with other teachers during my lunch break one or two days a week, since I'm out in a portable alone the rest of the day. I have a choir that meets during most lunch hours, and another that meets after school. These weekly lunch conversations have been my main connection to other teachers all year. I spend an extra hour at the end of the day to do my planning on these days so that I can spend lunch time with other teachers. (First-year junior high choral music teacher, Interview 1, 1999)

> I don't feel that I've found any mentors in this school or district in my first year of teaching; I've really had to wing it on my own. I rely primarily on past teachers for ideas and to discuss problems, since there is no mentor program in this district. There's no real team approach here for dealing with problems; you're pretty much expected to handle things on your own. (First-year middle school band teacher, Interview 7, 1999)

As described by these new music teachers, a lack of contact with other teachers can create a sense of intellectual isolation and a desire for peer support and collaboration. New teachers need to talk with other professionals who are familiar with their classroom situations as they interpret their new roles as teachers and try to make sense of student interactions.

Being assigned to several schools further increases isolation for some beginning music teachers, and often teachers with several school assignments do not identify with any one school faculty. Itinerant music teachers note that they frequently find themselves between schools during break times, are often scheduled to be at another school during faculty meeting times, and are often left out of decision making as a result. One beginning music teacher describes the situation:

> I don't see the rest of the middle school faculty very much; I try to go to staff meetings when I can, but they're held after school when I'm at the elementary schools. I try to make the middle school my home school, but I often have conflicts with meetings. (First-year grades 5–8 orchestra teacher, Interview 11, 1999)

Other itinerant music teachers similarly find that their schedules at multiple schools often further remove them from significant interactions with other teachers.

Some novice music teachers speak of a lack of contact specifically with other music teachers and of a need for music teacher mentors who have similar teaching assignments:

> We had new teacher facilitators, but they weren't music teachers. They couldn't help much with the problems I faced. The new teacher workshops we had occasionally were not at all focused on music problems, and I was the only music person in them. (First-year high school band teacher, Interview 9, 1999)

> You really need a mentor in your own building, as well as a music teacher mentor in your own area of teaching. Since I had neither, after the first few months of the school year I realized this, and I started going to the other special teachers in our school as resource people. I also started calling both the music teacher and my professor that I worked with during student teaching. (First-year general music teacher, Interview 2, 1999)

As described in this case, some new teachers eventually begin to build networks of support within their schools on their own initiative and for their own survival. Since it is not always realistic or possible for new teachers to find their own mentors and resource people when needed, how can schools create the structures and culture that enable new teachers to learn with and from other teachers as they begin to teach?

BEGINNING MUSIC TEACHER VIEWS ON EFFECTIVE MENTORING PROGRAMS

> I've been relying on the other two music colleagues at the high school a lot to answer my questions. These music teachers have really become my mentors because they're close by and open to questions. I seek them out and go to

them with almost everything when I need help. They help me to pay attention to following through and making sure kids are responding to my directions. (First-year middle/high school orchestra teacher, Interview 1, 2003)

Like other beginning professionals, new teachers need continuing opportunities to work under the guidance of more experienced professionals. Novice music teachers frequently say that they value collaboration and exchanges with experienced music teachers with assignments similar to their own. Most new music teachers view such links with other music teachers as essential to their learning and professional growth. Beginning music teachers who are offered the assistance of one or more experienced music teacher mentors describe situations that help them form further networks with other teachers. One music teacher describes her mentoring program:

> Our district does have a mentor program, and my mentor is the person who had been my cooperating teacher during student teaching. She has been a great sounding board and resource person. She always finds someone to help if my questions are outside of her experience or expertise, and she validates my decisions when I doubt myself.
>   We were also paid to observe experienced teachers for two full days, which was extremely valuable time. I could use several more observation days very effectively. We also had several weekend workshops given by the district for new teachers. These were excellent for sharing problems with other new teachers who might have different solutions to similar problems. We chose most of the issues discussed ourselves. (First-year middle school choral music teacher, Interview 14, 1999)

Rather than feeling isolated, this new music teacher had collaborative experiences that helped her find new perspectives and form further networks with other teachers.

Another new music teacher found herself struggling to understand the culture and background of the students in her very diverse, urban general music classroom. Though her preservice courses had theoretically prepared her in multicultural education, in her classroom she was now faced with understanding second language acquisition and student interactions that were at times perplexing and new to her. She noted:

> My mentor suggested that I take an in-service class on English as a second language. We read and talked about ways to help second language students, and I was able to observe how my mentor approached and interacted with these special needs students in music. This gave me ideas and routines to try as a starting point, and I was able to make progress in addressing this challenge in my own classroom. (First-year general music teacher, Interview 8, 2003)

By working with her music teacher mentor, this novice music teacher was able to learn second language approaches and teaching strategies and to discuss issues facing students with limited English proficiency in her general music classroom. Her mentor also served as a link to in-service opportunities and to a network of other teachers and resources.

New music teachers who had district-supported released days to visit other music teachers described these observations as a major source of ideas. One novice music teacher recalled:

> We had several days to visit other experienced teachers, and that has helped immensely. The teachers recommended to me were very gracious, and these observations provided me with lots of new ideas. (First-year high school choral music teacher, Interview 12, 1999)

Another noted:

> Our district allows one visit out of the building by the new teacher, and one visit by the mentor into the building. I did my visit at another MS band classroom, and that was very valuable. I'd like to do more visits. (First-year middle school band teacher, Interview 6, 2003)

New music teachers who received released time to observe other music teachers often found this experience to be of great assistance, as well as a means for establishing relationships with experienced music teachers. Seeing alternative ways of teaching can help beginning music teachers visualize new methods in their own practice. When mentors point out what they see as central in their own practice, they can assist novices to more fully interpret what they observe in the music classroom.

One novice music teacher described a monthly new teacher workshop offered by his district as part of a mentoring program:

> Besides my work with my mentor, our district has a class once a month for teachers new to the district, and we talk about things that the district feels are important to have in common philosophically, as well as discussing our own issues. I learned what the district is looking for in their teachers and met other new teachers in the district. It helped me strengthen some areas, such as getting my thoughts across to students. We also talked about issues like management philosophy and interacting with parents. (First-year general music teacher, Interview 11, 2003)

Another first-year teacher described her district's more extensive mentoring program, which she found very effective:

We had a mentor program which was great; we were paid for participating since the district had a grant, and new teachers could opt whether to partici- pate or not. We'd meet as a group of about a dozen, and we made our own agenda. We could then invite experienced teachers or administrators from the district to address the issues we wanted, and they were paid to participate. It was an excellent program and very beneficial to all of the new teachers, since we could voice our questions and problems and have them addressed. I was the only music teacher, but I got so many ideas from the other new teachers to use in my music classroom. It was also so helpful to have other new teachers to relate to about things that were happening the first year.

I had quite a bit of contact with other music teachers in the district, through phone conversations initiated by them and released time to observe them. We had three or four formal meetings during the year as a music staff. But the jun- ior high music teachers in the district made a point of checking in with me regu- larly, which was an enormous help when problems popped up. One experi- enced MS choral teacher in particular was a great and patient resource person and a source for borrowing music for my choirs. My professor from student teaching was also a primary resource person. (First-year junior high choral music teacher, Interview 3, 1999)

As noted by these new music teachers, a combination of district-supported men- toring by experienced music teachers, interactive workshops for new teachers addressing issues selected by them, and released time for observing experi- enced music teachers provided very effective collaborative practices. These interactions were viewed by new music teachers as providing effective assis- tance in addressing many of the problems they faced in their work, as a means for networking, and as a pathway for further personal and professional growth.

Although districts offered effective mentoring programs for only some of the new teachers studied, experienced music teacher mentors provided a positive impact and a wealth of resources when available. This finding suggests that beginning music teachers who have strong mentoring relationships with one or more music teachers experience less isolation than other novice music teach- ers. Beginning music teachers often rely heavily on other music teachers when they are available to them and speak of their absence when they are not. Mentoring relationships can enable new teachers to share materials, network, and find opportunities for professional growth such as music-specific workshops. Beginning music teachers are often able to think about their problems more creatively and gain confidence in their own practice through frequent interaction with other music teachers. One new music teacher illustrates this point:

I've been working in parallel with my mentor who is an experienced elementary music teacher ... Now I'm branching out and doing more of my own thing. My mentor was a great role model for curriculum and management, especially during the first few weeks of school. (First-year general music teacher, Interview 3, 2003)

This novice music teacher was able to make progress in establishing her own classroom practice with assistance from her mentor.

In summary, pairing new music teachers with mentors in similar teaching assignments, interactive workshops for new teachers addressing issues selected by them, and observations of experienced music teachers provided very effective collaborative programs for the new music teachers studied. Opportunities for novice teachers and their mentors to observe each other's classrooms and to confer with one another were effective ways of assisting the novice in becoming acclimated to classroom teaching. Mentorships appeared most effective when released time was provided for both mentors and new teachers, when several music mentors were available to interact with each novice, and when novices were paired with mentors in similar music positions and assignments. New teacher seminars or workshops proved beneficial when agendas were set by the participating teachers. Sharing concerns, ideas, and problems in these workshops was a positive support measure and an effective resource for most new music teachers.[8] Other sections in this book further outline current assistance programs and assessments of their effectiveness.

SUGGESTIONS FOR SUPPORTING BEGINNING TEACHERS

How do mentors approach mentoring? What types of mentoring interactions do beginning teachers find useful and supportive? What practices foster professional growth? New teachers indicate that they perceive interactions with other professionals as the most effective assistance during their initial years of teaching.[9] Mentoring has the potential to develop attitudes and skills for continuing growth or to reinforce status quo norms of noninterference. New teachers note that finding knowledgeable and willing mentors with compatible teaching styles is key to their successful professional growth during the first year of teaching. Schools and districts that acknowledge this finding are beginning to provide first-year teachers with a choice of mentors as part of a comprehensive induction program.

How can mentoring programs help to break the isolation of beginning teachers? New teachers often keep problems to themselves and can easily believe that challenges are somehow a failure or weakness. If teaching can be viewed within a school as a collective activity, new teachers can feel safe in sharing their difficulties and questions. One way to address the tendency of new teachers to withdraw might be to offer workshops for new teachers to meet and talk with each other. Along with engaging in unstructured conversations, experienced teachers can address specific issues designated by the new teachers. New teacher meetings along with mentoring activities can assist in creating support networks among new teachers.

Assessments of state mentoring programs have illustrated that preparing mentors has a significant impact on their ability to help new teachers. Mentoring programs often outline research-based strategies to foster inquiry-oriented guidance for beginning teachers. New studies are beginning to emerge that examine how mentors interact with new teachers. Feiman-Nemser[10] studied the practice of an experienced mentor and outlined the following approaches for fostering analytical thinking, self-confidence, and educational growth in new teachers:

- Seek out openings for dialogue.
- Pinpoint and reinterpret problems.
- Notice and acknowledge signs of growth.
- Explore the novice's thinking with questions.
- Think aloud about one's own educational decision-making processes.
- Model "wondering" about teaching.
- Focus the new teacher on students and student learning.

These approaches can assist new teachers in adjusting to new teaching situations and provide needed practical and emotional support. Mentors can be effective in the role of co-thinker and peer, brainstorming possible solutions to dilemmas rather than giving specific advice. New teachers need practice in talking about and analyzing their teaching in order to receive assistance from others. Wondering about teaching helps guide new teachers to ask questions about their teaching and can provide new ways of looking at challenges and problems. Asking questions to learn what new teachers meant by something they said may help them to make their ideas more clear. Focusing on students and student learning can help the new teacher to move beyond a novice's focus on self to seeing student progress in the classroom. Mentors who are analytical and self-evaluative about their own teaching can help novice teachers develop a reflective teaching practice of their own.

How does formal evaluation by administrators impact new teacher mentoring? New teachers are often hesitant to reveal their difficulties to administrators who will formally evaluate them. Concerns of novice teachers about formal evaluation suggest that mentors should maintain confidentiality about their observations and conferences and should not formally evaluate the beginning teachers with whom they work. Separating mentoring from formal evaluation allows new teachers to develop a sense of trust and openness with mentors and to feel safe in sharing the problems they face.

How are these mentoring strategies specifically helpful to new music teachers? One new music teacher described his experience:

> Being a teacher is a new role and a big responsibility. You need [a mentor] who knows you to tell you that you're doing things in a way that will work, because

half the time, you don't know. You make the best decisions that you can, but you don't have experience to draw upon to know what works and what doesn't. (First-year middle school band teacher, Interview 19, 2001)

Another first-year music teacher stated:

My mentor met with me extensively before the school year began and weekly for the first three months of school. We went over lesson plans and talked about issues that came up in my classroom. He helped me to analyze why something didn't go well and what to try doing about it. This really helped me to see what and how and why a master teacher does what he does ... to understand the difference between what kindergartners versus first graders can understand and do, and how to write a sequential curriculum. (First-year general music teacher, Interview 7, 2003)

These new music teachers' mentors provided guidance in building curriculum and in analyzing classroom problems, allowing new teachers to move forward in their own new directions and gain confidence in their own practice. Offering specific comments and feedback about accomplishments and what new music teachers are doing well gives them the confidence to move forward and address areas of difficulty. Since much of this dialogue is specific to music teaching, experienced music teacher mentors are invaluable in mentoring new music teachers.

OBSERVATION AND CONFERENCING

How might mentors structure observations with novice teachers? Observations and conferences are noted by many beginning teachers and mentors to be among the most effective practices for sharing strategies and information.[11] Classroom observations of the mentor by the new teacher are important to the novice, along with observations of the new teacher by the mentor. Glickman[12] suggests that interactive mentor/new teacher observations consist of three parts:

1. a pre-observation conference;
2. the observation itself; and
3. a post-observation conference.

During the pre-observation conference, the new teacher outlines the lesson goals and plan. One or two concerns or goals that the observer will watch for in the lesson are identified. During the observation, the observer takes notes on the goals identified in the pre-conference and records the teacher's exact words in reference to these. In doing so, the observer can avoid relying on memory or impressions alone.

At the post-observation conference, the new teacher is asked to analyze his or her perceptions with guidance from the mentor, describing what worked and concerns. The mentor focuses first on strengths of the lesson and then on the goals identified earlier. Specific examples from verbatim notes are provided concerning the designated goals. The mentor then guides the novice in determining potential actions or changes to be made. Questions that the mentor might ask the novice to initiate analysis might include:

- Think about your interactions with students, and evaluate your lesson. What went well? What might you do differently next time?
- Thinking about student goals, let's analyze the process of your lesson. Is your lesson evaluation consistent with student goals? How might you strengthen the continuity or clarity of lesson goals?

At the end of the post-observation conference, the new teacher is asked to summarize strengths, problems, and potential changes in the lesson.

When giving non-directive feedback and guidance, mentors might find the following actions helpful:[13]

- *Describing* rather than judging
- *Exploring* alternatives cooperatively rather than giving solutions (avoid saying, "I would have ... ")
- *Focusing*: Giving only the amount of feedback the teacher can realistically digest (one to three skills or goals at a time)
- *Listening* to and waiting for the teacher's initial statements and analysis
- *Reflecting* or paraphrasing the problems stated
- *Clarifying and questioning* underlying problems
- *Problem solving*: Asking the teacher to think of possible actions and to consider their consequences
- *Following through*: Asking the teacher to commit to a plan of action

Through this process, the mentor can encourage the new teacher to engage in self-analysis and approach his or her own instructional challenges in new ways.

These observation techniques and practices are examples of mentoring tools that foster inquiry-oriented professional development. Strategies that focus on student thinking and understanding, lesson planning, teaching diverse learners, motivating students, working with students who have special needs, and other issues can also be put to use by beginning teachers with help from mentors. Research-based and problem-oriented strategies are valuable resources for both new music teachers and their mentors.

As our teacher and student populations become more multicultural, we might learn to draw upon a multicultural perspective and on cooperative approaches to learning. One music educator tells us:

> Multicultural education invites a softening of the boundaries between teacher and student, suggesting that we can all learn from each other and can teach each other. Softening the boundaries creates an environment conducive to cooperative teaching and learning.[14]

As mentors work with new teachers, they can help novices explore and clarify their own unique teaching styles, backgrounds, and concerns. Collaborative teaching and learning is ever more needed in the teaching profession as our world becomes more diverse and encompasses a greater variety of backgrounds and learning styles.

Because teaching is complex and context dependent, it is important that mentoring programs avoid the confines of narrowly defined or prescribed lists of "standards" or "skills" to be mastered. Adjusting to and defining their new roles can be daunting for new teachers, even when novice teachers appear to be very successful and without evident classroom problems. New teachers need mentors they can trust who are willing to help them discover how they will define their own new roles and their identities as teachers. Mentors can be helpful in negotiating dilemmas and personal conflicts over new roles, which new teachers are often desperate to share and discuss with someone who is knowledgeable about their situation.

What might the impact of these mentoring interactions look like for new music teachers? One new music teacher described her first-year experience working with mentors:

> My previous cooperating teacher and university professor have been key mentors and role models for me. My principal has been helpful, also. These people are very proactive and make me feel that I can do things. They notice every little thing that I do well, and make the most of these. Even when there's a problem and things need to be changed, these people approach everything in a positive and proactive way, which has been very empowering for me. (First-year elementary orchestra and general music teacher, Interview 12, 2001)

Another novice music teacher described his interactions with mentors:

> I really relied on calling and meeting with several experienced music teachers whom I'd known previously ... They were a great help in providing positive reinforcement for me, for brainstorming ideas to solve problems, and for advice when asked. I invited one of my professors in to observe several times during the first month of school when things were really tough, and that was a big help. Sometimes you just need someone to tell you that you're on the right track and are making progress, because the progress is so slow and painful that it's hard to recognize yourself. (First-year middle school band teacher, Interview 19, 2001)

These new music teachers gained confidence and the ability to be proactive in approaching their own classroom problems through the support of experienced music teacher mentors.

CONCLUSION

As in other professions, new music teachers need consistent support from colleagues in order to be successful and prosper in the music education profession. By learning to search for new solutions to classroom problems, new teachers are allowed the risk of making mistakes and trying out new practices and solutions. Seeking new solutions as a way of life enables daily progress and continuing professional growth. Reminding novice teachers of their progress and encouraging them to trust in their eventual success helps them to work through difficult problems and challenging days.

As the new music teachers quoted in this chapter illustrate, the chance to connect with other music teachers is a powerful resource. Many new music teachers indicate that they would like to observe other teachers but rarely have the opportunity; providing chances to observe and confer with other music teachers can be an effective component of support programs. Networking with other music teachers, both new and experienced, can be a professional lifeline for beginning music teachers. Research suggests that collaboration and mentoring can increase self-confidence and motivation in new teachers.[15] New music teachers who have access to collaboration and effective support networks will be more able to gain the knowledge they need to become confident and competent educational decision makers and to meet the diverse needs of their students.

NOTES

1. Ellen Moir and Colleen Stobbe, "Professional Growth for New Teachers: Support and Assessment through Collegial Partnerships," *Teacher Education Quarterly* 22, no. 4 (1995): 83–91.

2. Linda Valli, "Beginning Teacher Problems: Areas for Teacher Education Improvement," *Action in Teacher Education* 14, no. 1 (1992): 18–25; Katherine Perez, Carole Swain, and Carolyn Hartsough, "An Analysis of Practices Used to Support New Teachers," *Teacher Education Quarterly* 24, no. 2 (1997): 41–52.

3. Mary Louise Gomez, "Reflections on Research for Teaching: Collaborative Inquiry with a Novice Teacher," *Journal of Education for Teaching* 16, no. 1 (1990): 45–56; Valli, "Beginning Teacher Problems."

4. Daniel Lortie, *School Teacher: A Sociological Study* (Chicago: University of Chicago Press, 1975).

5. Lisa DeLorenzo, "Perceived Problems of Beginning Music Teachers," *Bulletin of the Council for Research in Music Education,* no. 113 (1992): 9–25; Brent Sandene, "Determinants and Implications of Stress, Burnout, and Job Dissatisfaction among Music Teachers," *Update: Applications of Research in Music Education* 13, no. 2 (1995): 25–31;

Keith Thompson, "The Responsibilities and Needs of Beginning Music Teachers" (paper presented at MENC's National Conference, Indianapolis, 1988).

6. DeLorenzo, "Perceived Problems of Beginning Music Teachers."

7. Patti J. Krueger, "New Music Teachers Speak out on Mentoring," *Journal of Music Teacher Education* 8, no. 2 (1999): 7–13; Patti J. Krueger, "Reflections of Beginning Music Teachers," *Music Educators Journal* 88, no. 3 (2001): 51–54.

8. Krueger, "New Music Teachers Speak out on Mentoring."

9. Perez, Swain, and Hartsough, "An Analysis of Practices Used to Support New Teachers."

10. Sharon Feiman-Nemser, "Helping Novices Learn to Teach," *Journal of Teacher Education* 52, no. 1 (2001): 17–30.

11. Perez, Swain, and Hartsough, "An Analysis of Practices Used to Support New Teachers."

12. Carl Glickman, *Supervision of Instruction: A Developmental Approach* (Newton, MA: Allyn and Bacon, 1985); Carl Glickman, *Supervision of Instruction* (Needham Heights, MA: Allyn and Bacon, 1990).

13. Glickman, *Supervision of Instruction*, 1990.

14. Julia Eklund Koza, "Multicultural Approaches to Music Education," in *Making Schools Multicultural* (Englewood Cliffs: Prentice Hall, 1996), 276.

15. Sandra J. Odell and Douglas P. Ferraro, "Teacher Mentoring and Teacher Retention," *Journal of Teacher Education* 43, no. 4 (1992): 200–04.

Patti J. Krueger is professor and chair of music education in the School of Music at the University of Puget Sound.

Making Mentoring Work

Michael V. Smith

Mentor. It is an ancient and, at the same time, very modern word. Whether as distant as myth or as close as the next classroom, mentors provide guidance, instruction, encouragement, and nurturing. Mentors have been around for centuries, and both the term and concept continue to be widespread in a number of professions, including education.

Mention the word "mentor" to a business executive and he or she will, no doubt, be very familiar with it. It has become a popular and widely used expression in the professional world and generally refers to a person who "oversees the career and development of another person, usually a junior, through teaching, counseling, providing psychological support, protecting, and at times promoting or sponsoring."[1]

Say the word "protégé" or the more current term "mentee" to a person concerned with at-risk youth, and she or he too will probably respond with a nod of understanding. It suggests a person who receives personal assistance and support with the intent to nurture and advance that individual's chances for experiencing success. The mentor who shares concerns for at-risk youth recognizes that mentoring is an effective method for training and supporting new generations of young people and, at the same time, passing along some of the values and traditions developed by preceding generations.

Musicians also know these terms well. They bring to mind a method of instruction that is a rich part of music pedagogy tradition and, in fact, is an approach that continues to thrive in the studios and classrooms of many fine music schools and conservatories around the world.[2] For centuries, in Western as well as other cultures, aspiring composers, performers, and conductors have sought apprentice-like relationships with masters. Names such as Beethoven and Haydn, Brahms and Schumann, and Schöenberg and Berg are forever coupled together and linked in discussions of apprenticeships in compositional training and stylistic development. Performers such as Artymiew and Graffman, Cliburn and Lhevinne, and Ma and Stern are not only eminent examples of student-teacher associations but also cases in which mentors have offered the kind of sponsorship that is necessary for the successful launching of a performing career. Often intense, these relationships have been and continue to be the conduit through which many traditional performance practices as well as artistic and cultural values have been transmitted from one generation of musicians to the next.

As with their composing and performing counterparts, music educators also have identified masters within their profession. Orff, Kodály, Dalcroze, and Suzuki are well-known and venerated personalities in the discipline. Workshops and institutes bearing their names are common and usually very well-attended. These gatherings are often rich settings for sharing pedagogic concepts and strategies as well as lively places where teachers may find renewed energy for teaching music. But these events generally are not a substitute for the kind of ongoing, earnest, one-on-one relationships that generations of performers, conductors, and composers have long enjoyed and found to be beneficial. Music educators need and deserve this same kind of support because they too are expected to be proficient, model performers, conductors, educators, and at times even composers. The extensive investment made in preparing educators in terms of time and training, as well as the broad expectations and demands that their profession makes of them, warrants mentoring and guidance. This is particularly true of the music educators who frequently are licensed to teach from kindergarten through twelfth grade and often are the only music educator in a school. In addition, they are subject to a variety of public relations and performance responsibilities and have more complex program budget and administrative responsibilities than many other kinds of teachers.

Just how can music educators care for and support these individuals who are just beginning their careers? What strategies might be used to provide the kind of on-the-job, day-to-day support that these young teachers need and deserve? Many music educators, individually and with the assistance of state music associations, are turning to the promises offered by mentoring. The challenge is generally not in finding individuals who are willing to serve as mentors. Music educators are often caring and helpful and are typically willing to assist to the extent that their busy schedules will allow.

Rather, one of the primary challenges lies in equipping well-intentioned and concerned veteran music teachers with strategies that will prove to be effective methods for offering the support that new music teachers so badly need. In short, how can mentors offer effective help to new teachers, and how can young teachers find ways to receive that help?

A look at some of the historical and current principles and practices may help us identify and define some effective methods for a mentor to meaningfully support the professional life of a new teacher.

MENTOR ATTRIBUTES

As pointed out, mentoring is an important and historical concept. In fact, "if mentors did not exist," says Laurent Daloz, "we would have to invent them."[3] He goes on to say that they come in a variety of forms,

> from the grandmotherly fairy godmother to the elfin Yoda to the classic bearded Merlin. Myths, fairy tales, fantasy, and children's stories abound with the mentor figures: the spider woman in Native American lore, Gandalf in Tolkein, Charlotte in *Charlotte's Web*, Utnapishtim in the Gilgamesh epic, Shazam in Captain Marvel comics, the little old lady in *Babar*, Tiresias in Greek legend, the Skin Horse in *The Velveteen Rabbit*.[4]

One of the first allusions to a mentor occurs in Homer's epic poem *The Odyssey*. Odysseus, a distinguished and kingly warrior, was called to fight in the Trojan War. In his absence, his estate and, more importantly, his young son, Telemachus, were entrusted to the care of his friend and adviser, Mentor. Through the course of the story, Mentor guides Telemachus on a journey to find his father and, along the way, a new and fuller understanding of himself.

Eugene Anderson and Anne Shannon studied this relationship and maintain that this mythic partnership can be viewed as an archetype for good mentoring.[5] They offer several conclusions about the nature of mentoring based on the relationship of Mentor and his young charge, Telemachus. Their observations provide some framing principles that may help the music mentor who is seeking to support and nurture a novice music educator.

A MENTOR IS INTENTIONAL

First, effective mentoring should be intentional. Mentor carried out his duties toward Telemachus with a purpose and specific goals. Further, Odysseus did not leave it to chance that such a relationship would develop. He was proactive. He made the arrangements for Mentor to meet and know his mentee. And so Mentor and Telemachus entered into a relationship that allowed them to spend a generous amount of time together and that held many opportunities for the two to encounter both the challenges and joys of life together—because it was facilitated. And so it is today. One of my own mentors (who taught and *showed* me much of what it means to mentor) was fond of saying that each of us must *choose* to reach one; that each of us must *choose* to teach one. Mentoring is intentional and must be forged one relationship at a time.

So, individual mentors—or mentoring programs run by a school district or professional organizations—should reach out to young teachers. Facilitated, intentional efforts are key to developing successful mentoring relationships for several reasons. First, often, without facilitation, mentoring relationships just don't naturally develop. Young teachers are very busy and often overwhelmed with new responsibilities and activities. Given their new and full professional lives, they often do not have the extra drive to seek out a mentor on their own. In his book, *Biting the Apple*, Kevin Ryan offers a revealing and personal view of the life of the beginning teacher:

> For most, the first year is complex and difficult ... Most have just left the security and regularity of the campus; and while they may be eager to take on the world, it comes on them rather fast. They need to find a place to live and settle themselves into. For the first time in their lives they may need to purchase and maintain their own car. Some may be confronted with financial decisions for the first time: where to bank; how to handle checking accounts and credit cards; how to set up a budget and keep it. Many begin learning how to cook. There are dozens of new things to learn and connections to be made.[6]

Experienced teachers, too, are quite busy with the demands of their own successful professional lives. Full schedules and responsibilities can limit the likelihood that these generally well-meaning but often very active individuals will notice or intentionally make time for the questions and needs of a young colleague. Experienced teachers may be more likely to become involved when there is a program or system that supports and smooths the process of becoming a mentor.

A second reason to facilitate mentoring relationships grows out of human nature. Without the permission that a deliberate approach to a mentoring relationship brings, a mentor may feel reluctant to intrude or meddle in the younger teacher's professional practice. Conversely, without being given explicit permission to do so, a young teacher may not feel comfortable asking for help. Typically, music education mentors are successful and busy people. Without specific permission and encouragement to request help, a young teacher may feel her or his insecurities to be a nuisance to the veteran teacher and the inevitable stream of questions and concerns as an annoyance to the experienced mentor. An effective mentor gives the mentee explicit and absolute permission to approach him or her with any and all sorts of concerns. There should be an intentional freedom established and a spirit of kindness fostered that considers no mentee question too simple nor any concern too foolish. In this way, real-life issues can honestly emerge, be candidly discussed, and be effectively addressed.

A MENTOR IS NURTURING

Mentoring is a nurturing process that encourages the growth and maturity of the mentee. It was Mentor's responsibility to enable Telemachus to discover all that he was called to do and to become all that he was created to be. In short, Mentor and his young charge were called into a relationship. Certainly information needed to be shared. Guidance needed to be given. But, just as important, all was to be done in the context of a caring relationship.

A mentoring relationship is, in part, about sharing information and guidance. More fully, it should be a caring relationship. There is an old definition of mentoring that defines it well and in a quaint way. "A mentor," the saying goes, "is a brain to pick, a shoulder to cry on, and sometimes even a kick in the pants!" There are many dimensions to a healthy mentoring relationship, and, along with good information, nurturing is at the heart of what a mentee needs from a mentor. A listening ear and a caring heart are two of the most important things that a mentor can offer a mentee.

Many mentors and mentees have found that this sort of nurturing exchange happens quite powerfully and comfortably in the presence of food—a simple and perhaps obvious strategy. Breaking bread together somehow seems to allow us to feel comfortable to break open our lives to one another as well. Such a simple thing as sharing coffee together can be a powerful mentoring tool.

A MENTOR IS INSIGHTFUL

The relationship between Mentor and Telemachus was not without difficulties. Pointing out error was generally not Mentor's method of instruction. Rather, finding avenues by which Telemachus might discover his own mistakes and learn from them without becoming rebellious was the tack of the wise Mentor. Certainly there are moments when a young teacher needs prescriptive, practical, and even hands-on assistance. But, for a developing professional, there are often more times when the lesson needs to be learned through the experience of the trial or situation at hand. We do indeed learn by doing—and sometimes we learn by failing. And a mentor's tenderness in the wake of a tough learning experience can often lead to good conversation between mentor and mentee and go on to serve as a strong basis for growth and development.

A MENTOR IS SUPPORTIVE AND PROTECTIVE

Telemachus was to consider the words of Mentor seriously, and Mentor was, according to Homer's tale, to "keep all safe." These, then, are the two primary responsibilities and attitudes that the two people in this mentoring partnership bring to the relationship. First, the mentee must be willing to be open to the suggestions, observations, and instruction that the mentor offers. Second, the mentor must be certain that the relationship with the mentee is kept safe. Here are some suggestions for creating a healthy, supportive, and safe mentoring relationship:

Listen. Both the mentor and the mentee should genuinely listen. Para-phrasing one another (restating what the other has said) often helps bring clarity. Some have called this process "listening and resonating."[7] In short, the process involves listening to what the other person has to say, then responding in such a way that we echo or resonate the main idea the other person is expressing. Through this listening and resonating process, the listener allows the speaker to either confirm the thought shared or to correct and rephrase the idea so that both understand more clearly what was intended.

Use eye contact. Whether your eyes are focused on the speaker may signal, correctly or incorrectly, to what extent you are interested in or paying attention to what is being discussed.

Express warmth. When we show friendliness, use eye contact, or offer our hand in greeting, we express warmth. Such gestures are an enormous help in the development of a rapport that will foster genuine opportunities for sharing and, from there, occasions for professional growth.

Be honest. Once the relationship has been established as safe, any senti-ment, situation, or topic should be able to be openly and candidly discussed. This assumes that the mentor should not play a direct evaluative role in the professional life of the mentee. If the mentor does evaluate the mentee, then certainly some of the safe boundaries that are essential to a full and healthy mentoring relationship will be compromised. The role of evaluator can so easily threaten and even trump the role of mentor. Safety, trust, and candor do not easily persist in the presence of judgement and performance reviews. Confi-dentiality within the mentoring relationship should also be discussed, and agreements about those boundaries should be clearly defined.

A MENTOR IS A ROLE MODEL

According to the legend, the true identity of Mentor was that of Athena, the goddess of war and wisdom. In order to effectively provide Telemachus with a style and standard of behavior that he could understand, she took a human form, which he could readily perceive. Such an outward appearance also allowed for accessibility. Mentees can look to role models for perspective, style, and a sense of empowerment.

Beyond this mythic archetype and role model, there is research that seems to indicate the mentees prefer to work with a mentor who is like them profes-sionally. Gender, age, and experience appear to be less a factor than experi-ence and expertise within a specific area and level of the music curriculum.[8] For example, junior high or middle school mentees tend to find high school mentors less helpful than a mentor who also teaches at the junior high school level. A familiarity with current grade-specific teaching techniques and materials seems to be an important characteristic of the most effective mentor-mentee matches.

A MENTOR IS AFFIRMING

As Levinson[9] and others have noted, mentees often enter into new stages of professional or personal development with only a vague sense of their potential or identity. They may have only an indistinct vision for their future and an imagined perception of possibilities that generates enthusiasm and vigor. Giving that dream greater definition and finding ways to help the mentee live it out is another role the mentor plays. Without such support, Levinson suggests that the dream will remain unconnected to the mentee's life and may, as a result, simply die. The mentor offers life to the mentee's dreams and potential through words and actions of affirmation, just as Mentor spoke words of hope about the future to Telemachus:

> Not the least shyness, now Telemachus. You came across the open sea for this—to find out where the great earth hides your father and what the doom was that he came upon ... Reason and heart will give you words, Telemachus, and a spirit will counsel others. I should say the gods were never indifferent to your life.[10]

We all need individuals—mentors—who will make a commitment to watch over us, help us build our lives, be available and accessible to us, and most importantly, affirm us in our growth and development. There is a simple, old saying that answers an equally simple and old question: "When does a man become a man? Not until his father tells him he is." The same goes for a woman and her mother. And the same goes, to some extent, for the novice music educator who needs a similar sort of affirmation from another music educator whom he or she admires and respects. The novice teacher needs a mentor, someone who can identify and name the qualities and abilities within emerging professional practice and can characterize the young teacher as a competent and capable professional. Affirmation is a key function of mentoring and should be an intentional part of the ongoing relationship.

A MENTOR NEEDS MENTORS

None of us makes it alone. As one of my mentors used to say to me, we "each one reach one; we each one teach one." And that goes for mentors too. The development of the noble list of character attributes that we have been considering takes time, effort, and investment. We each need the assistance of a whole constellation of individuals who are willing to help us build our lives before we have the wherewithal to do the same for another. Mentors need mentors and peers who will offer them continuing support. Mentors need to continue to grow, both personally and professionally. To that end, ongoing training in such topics as collegial supervision, adult learning, and peer supervision, as well as just conversation with other mentors, may prove to be beneficial for mentor development and, in turn, in the developing lives of their mentees.

Finally, we need to be realistic. After all, no one but a mythical Mentor could ever be expected to fully measure up to the list of attributes that we have been considering. We are, after all, only human. But we can make effort to grow and to develop these qualities and, perhaps in the process, find that we can indeed begin to help another develop as a professional.

MATCHING MENTORS AND MENTEES

Along with specific mentor qualities, there are some other criteria that should be considered when creating mentoring pairs. These are practical matters, and they should not be overlooked when attempting to facilitate good mentor-mentee pairings.

The level and area of instruction of the mentor should match that of the mentee. In other words, mentees who teach middle school should have a mentor who also teaches middle school—someone who is viewed as understanding the challenges and opportunities of that particular instruction level. Elementary general music teachers should work with a mentor who also teaches elementary general music, right down to the same grade levels—intermediate general music, for instance, is seen as not as good a match for a primary general music teacher as is another K–3 music teacher.

Because music teachers are often the only music instructors in their building, administrators will often assign that new teacher to a mentor who is in the same building but who teaches in another curricular area. An experienced algebra teacher, for example, may be assigned to mentor the new band director. Some good and general assistance may come from such a pairing. School procedures, general teaching principles, and the like may be profitably shared and discussed. Yet there remain some fundamental and rather extraordinary differences between the methods and procedures of instruction in these two types of classrooms. (Picture the contrast between quiet desk work and a marching band rehearsal!) Even though the choir director across the hall from this new band director may be able to offer some good guidance, findings coming out of such programs as the Yamaha Project 2000 Mentoring Program[11] indicate that, for the best mentor-mentee pairing, that new high school band director would best profit from the assistance of another high school band director.

The mentor should be available and accessible to the mentee. Good teachers make good mentor candidates—but only if they are able to make the commitment and take the time to be easily reached. This can present a challenge for the busy and in-demand mentor. Typically, along with school obligations, successful teachers often hold positions of responsibility in professional organizations, other musical groups, and are active in a number of other professional pursuits. Working with a mentee is a commitment that will require making realistic and intentional choices about some of these other professional priorities.

The mentor should have good interpersonal skills. Good communication skills are a must for good mentoring. There are times when a mentor needs to be direct and prescriptive in offering the mentee the help that he or she needs. There are many times, however, when it will be more important to be a good colleague who listens. Being a mentor is in large part about sharing insights and offering constructive advice; knowing how to do this effectively and tactfully is key. Mentoring is also and perhaps in equal measure about offering emotional support, and being a good listener is a great place to start.

Novice teachers need good stress-management strategies. They need to learn how to cope with the inevitable negative conversations that will be heard in and around schools among other faculty and administrators. Less than positive encounters with parents, administrators, or other teachers are bound to happen. Listening thoughtfully and offering a knowing and sensible point of view is a significant part of what a mentor can provide to a new professional.

Mentors must also realize that mentees should be given the space that they need to grow and to make mistakes and learn on their own. Good teachers know that readiness is central to the teachable moment. And so do good mentors. Patience and common sense are two powerful mentoring strategies— recognizing what is an urgent situation and what is not, and taking the time to allow mentoring moments to emerge from the mentee's own questions or predicaments.

Mentors and mentees should be allowed some room for self-selection. Though the relationship can be facilitated, too much control of pairing runs the risk of going against the grain of the personal preferences and the good "chemistry" that is necessary for a healthy mentoring relationship to develop. For this reason, it is wise to allow mentors and mentees to meet and make individual choices about whom they would feel most comfortable forming a relationship with. Project 2000 participants found that this worked very well in the context of an informal dinner. Illinois and Minnesota music educators (IMEA and MMEA) continue to make such connections possible at their state conferences through a new teacher breakfast.

The mentor should know how to observe and coach. Techniques for looking in on a music lesson or rehearsal and then offering collegial guidance should be developed. Carl Glickman suggests that there are two parts to the observation process.[12] First, the observer describes, in nonjudgmental ways, what has been seen and heard. Second, *and with the input of the mentee*, the mentor and mentee interpret and discuss the lesson or rehearsal. A collegial approach to both aspects—describing and then interpreting—is crucial to the success of a mentoring relationship. Briefly, here are three simple tools that a mentor might use to observe and coach.

First, the mentor can count. Almost any facet of a rehearsal or classroom can be isolated and counted. For example, through observation (either from a live, in-person visit or from a videotape) the mentor can note how many times students ask for a hall pass. The number is tallied and, during a later conversation between mentor and mentee, the number is presented. If it is deemed an inordinately high number, the conversation can naturally lead to the "why" behind the number and then perhaps to a meaningful discussion of underlying pedagogical or other issues. In other words, the hall pass issue is really only the presenting symptom. The analysis of the situation may lead to deeper and more important teaching and learning matters and diagnoses.

Second, the mentor can diagram. Figure 1 illustrates such a strategy. The arrows in the figure represent verbal exchanges between the teacher and the different sections of a school ensemble. Arrows have been drawn to indicate to whom the comments were directed and in which directions they were made. Some interesting interpretations might be drawn from this visual representation of the rehearsal. For example, noting that most of the teacher's comments are directed toward the trombone section, the mentor might surmise that the director is a trombone player and, true to stereotype, favors his own section during a rehearsal. Or, perhaps those particular moments of the rehearsal were focused

FIGURE 1. DIAGRAM EXAMPLE OF VERBAL INTERACTION

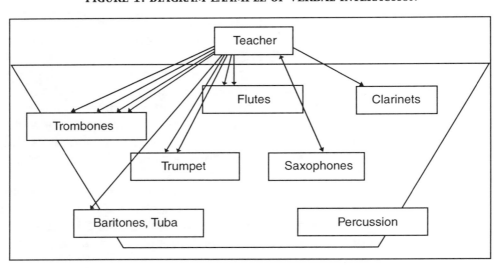

on an especially treacherous stretch of music for the low brass. The mentor must allow the mentee the opportunity to reflect and perhaps explain. Whatever the case, some helpful insights might emerge from the presentation of this data, particularly when the mentor also points out the remarkable lack of comments directed toward the percussion section—certainly a recipe for disaster in any band director's book!

A third observation tool that a mentor might use is to record. Some observation models refer to this as *verbatim*. The mentor takes careful notes, writing down all interactions that take place in the classroom. Using abbreviations and leaving out words here and there is rather like creating a transcript of the lesson or rehearsal. While the process can be burdensome, it can also prove to be most helpful in identifying patterns in the novice teacher's classroom. Videotape is a wonderful tool for capturing a transcript of a rehearsal or lesson, especially when the camera is not left static and focused only on the teacher. (A colleague might be recruited to run the camera.) "The camera never blinks," as the saying goes, and the videotape of a class can add a measure of objectivity in the later discussion and interpretation of the dynamics of a lesson or rehearsal. The mentor can also turn the procedure and the camera around and, on occasion, record his or her own rehearsals for the purpose of modeling for the mentee—a terrific idea, particularly when the mentee has limited opportunity to make in-school observations.

Counting, diagramming, and recording are but three proven and effective observation strategies. Clinical supervision and teacher development literature can be explored for many more techniques.

Not all mentors need be multiyear veterans. Consider the possibility of including second-year teachers in the mentoring relationship. The creation of "mentoring triads" was one of the strongest components to emerge from the experimental Project 2000 program. By extending the mentoring relationship beyond one year, another first-year teacher can be invited into the mentoring pair, which now becomes a mentoring triad that includes a mentor, a first-year teacher, and a second-year teacher.

First-year teachers gain from the larger perspectives that the mentor continues to bring to the mentoring triad. Having just survived their own rookie year, second-year teachers also can contribute what is often very practical and helpful guidance for the first-year teacher. Of course, they also continue to receive support from the mentor for a more extended period of time. Further, the second-year member of the mentoring triad is given the opportunity to begin to develop a sense of professional competence as he or she discovers that, after only one year, he or she has indeed grown and has things to share that will help build the professional life of another young teacher. The mentor has the opportunity to be reenergized by the professional life of not one, but two young colleagues.

MENTORING STYLES: HOW TO OFFER HELP

Fundamentally, mentoring is a helping relationship. In education, the mentor is friend, guide, counselor, but above all, teacher. Mentors and teachers assist in various ways and, at the same time, learners and mentees prefer to be taught in various ways. Through the facilitated relationships between mentors and mentees in such programs as Project 2000, a dynamic quality about how people prefer to give and receive professional help is becoming evident. As the younger member of the pair is led from dependence to independence, from learning to make it in the "real world" to developing a vision for an "ideal world," certain shifts take place in the relationship. I have come to appreciate a model developed by William and Marilynne Gray.[13] It crystallizes what appear to be different levels in the fluid life of a mentoring relationship. In a broader sense, these mentoring styles might also be aptly applied to the relationship between any learner and teacher. The diagram on page 88 traces a maturing process in which the mentor brings a mentee (or protégé) alongside and shepherds that individual from a place of dependence to a point of independence. Initially, the relationship focuses on short-term goals and the development of particular competencies that the newcomer needs in order to survive and become an effective teacher. Gradually, however, horizons are broadened and the job of equipping the mentee (or protégé) to meet the challenges of short-term goals gives way to the task of empowering that individual to function independently and successfully with less need of the mentor's assistance. So, more specifically, how does this relationship grow? Let's look at each level more closely.

LEVEL ONE: THE MENTOR AS TEACHER

"Where do I go to find music for my middle school band?" "I have some elementary kids who are confused about trying to match pitches with my male voice. How can I help them?" "How do I take care of taking attendance, making announcements, warming up the choir, and generally getting my choral rehearsals off to a smooth start?" Fledgling teachers can be overwhelmed by the seemingly hundreds of questions that were not covered in methods classes. Having an experienced colleague to whom they can turn and ask for practical solutions to the very real challenges of daily classroom life can be, at the least, helpful. At most, it can be a matter of survival.

Mentors can effectively begin to address these needs by inviting the mentee to come and observe them in their own classroom situations. Though not a new idea, it is still quite a sound one. Just as the apprentice first watches the master, so the young music teacher is invited to observe and notice, with a vision made keen by a new recognition of his or her own needs, just how the mature teacher handles these same challenges and effectively creates opportunities for learning. Again, at this level the need is immediate, and the help given needs to be straightforward and immediate. At this point, the mentor says, in effect, "Watch what I do."

LEVEL TWO: THE MENTOR AS COACH

"Now, you do it and I'll watch." This is the next logical step in the helping relationship. Seeing that the mentee is growing in experience and capabilities, the mentor can now step to the sidelines and offer suggestions and observations rather than prescriptions and models. As the pair moves to the mentee's own classroom, the younger music teacher is given the opportunity to practice under the sharp and caring eye of an experienced practitioner. Instructional routines may be reviewed and teaching materials considered with the help of a seasoned perspective.

There are two points to be made here. First, it is still appropriate for the mentor to lead the discussion, although the role is now one of persuading rather than prescribing. In this model, leading questions may be framed and alternative approaches may be suggested, but it is the responsibility of the mentee to decide how to act and implement such suggestions. For example, rather than making a comment such as, "Speak up—the percussion section gets restless because they can't hear you," the mentor may lead the mentee to just such a realization by posing a more open-ended question. Asking, "Why do you suppose the students in the percussion section seemed to wander off-task while you were giving instructions?" may lead to the same conclusions as the first comment, but responsibility for such a realization begins to be subtly shifted from the mentor to the mentee. Second, it is important to note that, though the eye of the mentor is sharp, the comments are not. In fact, if the mentor is to be effective, then he or she must be viewed as supportive, caring, and free of any evaluative agenda. Certainly weaknesses are identified and areas for improvement are discussed, but such conversation takes place in a context that seeks to nurture and promote confidence and growth.

LEVEL THREE: THE MENTOR AS COLLABORATOR

This level of interaction marks a transition point in the mentoring relationship. The mentee is now capable of carrying out tasks and solving problems in a much more independent manner. As a result, the mentor must learn to become less dominating. True collegiality between peers is not yet appropriate, but a shift to a progressively more independent stance on the mentee's part is. Interaction between the pair is characterized by brainstorming and other methods of sharing that allow for both partners to contribute their thoughts and experiences in a true give-and-take fashion.

Music from a new materials reading session, for example, might be passed back and forth between the pair as they look at ideas and suggestions for applications for both teachers. Or perhaps both have been trying out a new listening lesson that they have developed together and are now using in their own classes. Together they sit down and talk through what does and does not work for them in the lesson. Though the relationship between the two is not completely on equal footing, it is certainly moving in that direction.

LEVEL FOUR: THE MENTOR AS SPONSOR

By this stage, mentees have become nearly self-sufficient but still look to the mentor for confirmation and encouragement. An important new role that the mentor comes to play at this level is that of connecting the mentee to the larger professional network. As the established professional, the mentor has the opportunity to sponsor the younger educator by making introductions to other members of the professional community and perhaps even making recommendations for opportunities in professional organizations and so forth. Playing such a role can be a key factor in the health of not only a particular career but also of the profession in general.

LEVEL FIVE: THE MENTOR AS COUNSEL

At this point the relationship becomes redefined in collegial terms. Having grown in competence and independence, the younger educator now relies on the experienced teacher more for career perspective than for methodological ideas. Also, the former mentee is now poised to become a new mentor and is capable of reinvesting the time and effort that his or her own mentor provided him or her. The mentee is now prepared to make a commitment to begin helping a less experienced new colleague.

So, the mentoring cycle continues and, as can be seen, is far from terminal. It is quite germinal, as care for the young educator bears fruit in the form of more effective instruction right now and, just as important, in the planting of seeds for the future able leadership of the profession. In addition, there is the potential to cultivate a rich and rewarding relationship between generations of teachers that can be beneficial and satisfying for both members of the mentoring pair.

PROFESSIONAL DEVELOPMENT FOR CAREER GROWTH

A mentor begins by helping a beginning teacher survive the first year of teaching, continues to support the mentee as he or she strives for growing competence and professional assurance through the following years, and finally, we hope, the mentor sees the mentee begin to thrive in a long and successful career as a music educator. A mentor can initiate career planning that can assist in the launching of a thriving career. Paul Haack has developed a mentor-guided formal and systematic process for such lifelong growth and advancement. His Professional Development Plan (Figure 2) may be helpful in guiding conversations around the continued career needs and goals of the mentee. Haack notes that "a professional development plan is a living, evolving document, subject to constant review, evaluation and change."[14] With that thought in mind, here is his suggested outline of procedures for guiding the process of professional career planning and development.

FIGURE 2. PROFESSIONAL DEVELOPMENT PLAN

A Construct for Balanced Development

Institutional Professional Development
(School Expectations and Needs)

Individualized Professional Development
(Personal Interests and Needs)

Personal Examples

Becoming knowledgeable about local policies and state mandates affecting music programs and education.

Serving in a specific capacity on the board of the state music educators association.

Intellectual

Continuing to pursue new directions of learning in the arts and social sciences and interdisciplinary learning.

Developing expertise in a related field with applications to music, e.g., electronics.

Musical

Furthering knowledge of theory, musicology, or ethnomusicology.

Developing improvisation skills; composing and publishing music.

Instructional

Gaining competence in special music education and/or music therapy to work better with exceptional children.

Gaining competence to serve as a supervisor of student teachers and/or a mentor of teachers.

Note: This Professional Development Plan is based on materials from the MENC Teacher Education Task Force report, *Music Teacher Education: Partnership and Process* (Reston, VA: MENC, 1987) and the Yamaha Project 2000 research report, "Project 2000: Mentoring and Professional Development—The Minnesota Model." Reprinted, with permission, from Michael V. Smith and Paul Haack, "The Long View of Lifelong Learning," *Music Educators Journal* 87, no. 3 (2000), 30–33.

Continued on next page

FIGURE 2 CONTINUED

The Long View

INSTITUTIONAL/PROFESSIONAL		PERSONAL/PROFESSIONAL
_____	By age 25	_____
_____	By age 35	_____
_____	By age 45	_____
_____	By age 55	_____
_____	By retirement	_____
_____	After retirement	_____

Goal Setting

My Professional "Wish List"

In three to five years I want to ...

In five to ten years I want to ...

Goal Analysis

Discuss the completed "wish list" with your mentor and formulate appropriate items into realistic goals.

Three- to five-year goals
Personal:
Intellectual:
Musical:
Instructional:

Five- to ten-year goals
Personal:
Intellectual:
Musical:
Instructional:

Discuss these goals a little further and attempt to prioritize them (high, medium, low).

FIGURE 2 CONTINUED

Needs Determination and Prioritization

Discuss your strengths and your needs with your mentor in terms of what you require to achieve each of your goals. Write them in the appropriate goal area spaces.
(If this activity brings to mind additional goals of importance, go back and add them to the Goal Setting form.)

Goal Areas	Strengths and Assets	Needs to Attain My Goals
Personal		
Intellectual		
Musical		
Instructional		

Take a few minutes to review and prioritize your needs.

FIGURE 2 CONTINUED

Goal Attainment Strategies

Enter goals below, in priority order if possible. Where helpful, include objective, sub-goals, or stepping-stones needed to reach goals. Note the necessary means and resources required to attain goals and objectives, and give realistic timelines and deadlines.

Goals/Objectives	Means and Resources (Needs)	Timelines

WHY BE A MENTOR?

Mentoring can be a rewarding and professionally enriching experience. It is gratifying to be able to help a new colleague learn and grow in his or her chosen profession. At the same time, the mentor may also find that he or she also gains from the experience. A mentee can bring a breath of fresh air into a longtime music educator's professional life. Often there is a fair trade of youthful creative energy and idealism for wisdom and experience. New ideas from academia are allowed to interact with experience in terms of what really works and what doesn't. The mentor may discover that the younger professional brings new energy and even novel new perspectives to the mentor's years of professional practice. In addition, being selected as a mentor can enhance self-esteem, serve as recognition of professional competence, and generally motivate a seasoned teacher to continue to grow and to set new and higher professional goals. Some programs may provide for financial rewards, though in the field of education these tend to be minimal.

The primary incentive for mentoring is normally not monetary. The strongest motives for mentoring a young colleague are often the same motives that persuade us to teach in the first place. They are motives based on desires to help another person to grow in competence and realize his or her full potential. Larry Ambrose puts it this way:

> Good mentors inspire their mentees to learn and grow; to see new things and new possibilities not only in their jobs, but in themselves. Sometimes the very fact of having a mentor will give individuals confidence enough to move into new areas of experience and make harder decisions involving both themselves and others.[15]

All music educators need to find ways that will renew, refresh, and affirm their practice—the press of daily teaching responsibilities demand it, if we are to continue to enjoy a healthy professional and even personal life. Being a mentor can be one of the ways to accomplish this. It may truly be that, in giving to young professionals, we come to discover that we receive more than we invest and that, as they grow and thrive, so do we.

NOTES

1. Michael G. Zey, *The Mentor Connection* (Homewood, IL: Dow-Jones Irwin Press, 1984).
2. Henry Kingsbury, *Music, Talent, and Performance* (Philadelphia: Temple University Press, 1988).
3. Laurent Daloz, *Mentor: Guiding the Journey of Adult Learners* (San Francisco: Jossey-Bass, 1999).
4. Ibid.

5. Eugene Anderson and Ann Shannnon, "Toward a Conceptualization of Mentoring," *Journal of Teacher Education* 39, no. 1 (1988): 38–42.

6. Kevin Ryan, *Biting the Apple, Accounts of First Year Teachers* (New York: Longman Press, 1980).

7. Paul Welter, *How to Help a Friend* (Carol Stream, IL: Tyndale Press, 1978).

8. Michael V. Smith, "The Mentoring and Professional Development of New Music Educators: A Descriptive Study of a Pilot Program" (Ph.D. diss., University of Minnesota, 1994).

9. Daniel Levinson, *The Seasons of a Man's Life* (New York: Ballantine, 1986).

10. Homer, *The Odyssey*, trans. R. Fitzgerald (New York: Doubleday, 1961).

11. Smith, "The Mentoring and Professional Development of New Music Educators."

12. Carl Glickman, *Supervision and Instructional Leadership: A Developmental Approach* (New York: Allyn and Bacon, 2000).

13. William and Marilynne Gray, "Synthesis of Research on Mentoring Beginning Teachers," *Educational Leadership* 43, no. 3 (1985).

14. Smith, "The Mentoring and Professional Development of New Music Educators," 264.

15. Larry Ambrose, *A Mentor's Companion* (Chicago: Perrone-Ambrose Press, 1998).

Michael V. Smith is associate professor and chair of music education at DePaul University in Chicago.

Part IV:
Critical Issues

Assistance Versus Assessment

Mitchell Robinson

> How we treat the least experienced among us is a reflection of how we feel about ourselves as a profession. The importance given to induction is a barometer of our professional self-esteem.[1]

> Novices have two jobs to do—they have to teach and they have to learn to teach.[2]

Many of our profession's leading thinkers believe that the issue of beginning teacher induction and support should be thought of less as a point between college and employment than as a continuum straddling preservice preparation and the first years of in-service experience and development. Beginning teacher induction and support, therefore, is not an event, but a developmental phase. This phase is characterized by a number of *critical tensions* that serve to illustrate the complicated, complex nature of teaching as a profession and the sometimes overwhelming challenges often faced by our least-experienced colleagues.

BACKGROUND

The education profession has struggled with the thorny issue of assistance versus assessment[3] of beginning teachers for nearly forty years. Part of our difficulty in negotiating the apparent dichotomy between supporting and evaluating new teachers may lie with our definitions of "induction." Many induction programs across the country, for example, are built around the somewhat limited notion of helping beginning teachers during their first year on the job and are focused on vague ideas of "support" or "assistance."

Indeed, such programs attempt to actively distinguish themselves from two other activities—"orientation meetings for beginning teachers and formal evaluation programs."[4] The separation, however, between assistance and assessment or evaluation is still a source of major tension and debate within the profession.

The traditional position held by many educators is that support and evaluation are incompatible or mutually exclusive functions that should not be included in the same program or conducted by the same persons. Teacher evaluation has historically been an administrative responsibility, while "according to conventional wisdom, mentors should assist not assess on the grounds that novices are more likely to share problems and ask for help if mentors do not evaluate them."[5]

Meanwhile, some in the profession[6] are calling for a rather more robust approach to induction that incorporates multiple functions, such as training and assessment. The need for training is partly in response to the increased numbers of new teachers entering the profession through alternate routes to certification. (For example, in Connecticut, the State Department of Education's "Alternate Route to Certification" [ARC] program is now the state's largest provider of newly certified music teachers, producing more new teachers than all of the state's collegiate music teacher education programs combined.) In these cases, the traditional boundaries between collegiate teacher preparation and in-service induction become blurred.

The traditional position has also been challenged by reformers who consider the formative assessment of beginning teachers as fulfilling both *bridging* and *gate-keeping* functions. More states are now incorporating both functions in their induction initiatives (e.g., California's "Beginning Teacher Support and Assessment" [BTSA] program and Connecticut's "Beginning Educator Support and Training" [BEST] program), while several large urban school districts (e.g., Toledo, Rochester, Cincinnati, and Columbus) have designed programs for beginning teachers around a peer assistance and review model that involves "consultant teachers" who provide assistance and make recommendations about continued employment. The latter initiatives are tied to "career ladder" programs for teachers, which were negotiated into teacher contracts during a previous reform movement in the late 1980s and early 1990s. As these programs demonstrate, the apparent dichotomy between assistance and assessment of new teachers that formed the core of previous thinking about induction has been significantly adapted over time, challenging us to reconsider our notions of how to bring new music teachers into the profession.

In addition to the philosophical dissonance between the ideas of assisting and assessing new teachers, there is also disagreement over how best to structure any possible interactions between the two components. According to Feiman-Nemser,[7] three combinations are possible:
1. support separated from assessment;
2. support integrated with formative assessment; and
3. support integrated with both formative and summative evaluation.

CAUTIONS

Any consideration of merging the constructs of assistance and assessment requires a few cautionary words. First, it should be understood that the evaluation of beginning teachers should be conducted along disciplinary lines; that is, a "one size fits all" approach fits no one at all. It is troubling, for example, that of the thirty-eight states that offer some kind of program targeted towards novice teachers,[8] only one state—Connecticut—provides an evaluation program based on subject-specific standards instead of generic sets of teaching skills and criteria that are applied across disciplines. Huber endorses this view of teaching as a discipline-specific endeavor:

> [The Carnegie Academy for the Scholarship of Teaching and Learning] program is built on the premise that these should be disciplinary communities, in part because of the importance of the disciplines to a scholar's academic identity, and also because teaching is not a generic technique, but a process that comes out of one's view of one's field and what it means to know it deeply.[9]

This is not to imply that there is nothing to be gained by considering the act of teaching and learning in a broader, cross-disciplinary manner. Huber continues, noting that each discipline, in developing its own scholarship of teaching and learning, may be able to contribute to a larger effort:

> Carnegie is also committed to the value of conversation and exchange among the disciplines as a way of building and strengthening the cadre of instructors in and around the academy who are committed to exploring teaching and learning as part of their teaching practice.[10]

Linking assessment and assistance can prove stressful to many teacher mentors, even if they are *not* supportive of their mentee's entry into the profession. Mentors need a comprehensive program of support, counseling, and training to negotiate this new terrain. Personally, I was very uncomfortable with the idea of linking assistance and assessment of new teachers until I began to consider who actually was making the decisions on teacher licensure and continued employment. When I was a beginning music teacher, the school board and administrators in my district had the sole responsibility for "making the call" on my continued employment; none of those administrators had music backgrounds, and not one member of the board had ever attended college. In retrospect, how meaningful was their decision on my career at that time, regardless of how they voted?

In Connecticut's BEST program, these important decisions are being made by veteran music teachers using a portfolio-based assessment model. The data collected in the portfolio include videos of teaching and supporting documentation that addresses issues of instructional planning, teaching techniques and strategies, assessment practices, and reflective thought and writing on the part of the beginning teacher. The school board members who held my career in their hands took a straw vote, basing their decision largely on the results of a handful of required observations, usually conducted hastily by principals or vice principals who were primarily concerned with my classroom management skills.

Assistance in my formative years as a music educator was limited to informal chats with whatever experienced music teachers I could find in my area; mostly, I was left to figure out teaching on my own, with my students. The first-year teachers I work with now have a variety of resources to turn to for support, including their BEST mentor, a building mentor, "Beginning Teacher Buddies," college professors, BEST Teachers-in-Residence, and a series of BEST training seminars during their first two years of service. While we do not know if the seminars are helping beginning teachers pass the portfolio assessment, we do know that those who fail the measure are among the least likely to attend the seminars.

EDUCATORSHIP + MUSICIANSHIP = MUSIC EDUCATORSHIP

Indeed, there is a common core of teaching that holds across disciplines—things such as understanding how students learn, develop, and differ in their approaches to learning, proficiency in one's content area, knowing how to design and deliver instruction, classroom management and communication skills, using various assessment techniques to evaluate student learning and modify instruction as appropriate, and engaging in self-evaluation and reflective practice in service of lifelong learning over the course of one's career. This set of core skills and competencies might be thought of as "educatorship." There is also a core set of skills within the discipline of music (e.g., music theory and history, keyboard and aural skills, applied study, and ensemble experience) that may be thought of as contributing to one's "musicianship."

While both skill sets are important, neither is sufficient on its own to prepare one for entry into the music education profession. Further, these skills are best learned in tandem, producing through their interaction what we might think of as "music-educatorship," allowing the learner to spiral back and forth between educational and musical content, and applying the principles learned in a mutually informing manner.

Assessing the development of music-educatorship in beginning teachers is a complex, complicated endeavor. For this reason alone, it requires the participation of skilled, experienced music teachers who are conversant in a variety of methodological approaches and who are aware of the issues, pressures, and challenges that confront beginning music teachers. Further, this group of potential evaluators must undergo extensive training in assessment techniques and strategies to ensure that the assessment process is valid and consistent for every novice teacher.

The consideration of training should not be limited to the assessors; in-service training should also be an important component of any beginning teacher assessment initiative, with content- or discipline-specific training sessions offered both before and after the evaluation period. High-stakes testing without diagnostic evaluation leading to remedial or compensatory in-service training and professional development serves a less than useful purpose in terms of maintaining and improving the teaching workforce. If the major goal of evaluation is the improvement of instruction, then it follows that the primary objective of assessing the quality of new teachers should be to diagnose problems, prescribe solutions, and improve beginning teachers' abilities to engage their students in meaningful music learning.

Building a diagnostic component into the assessment procedure also helps to improve the validity of the entire process by ensuring that the elements of teaching that are judged inadequate are properly identified and agreed upon and appropriate recommendations are made for improvement. Another complicating factor in this discussion are the competing forces of the teacher shortage and ongoing work to enhance the quality of the teaching workforce by raising standards and reexamining preservice teacher preparation.

While early reports advocated the separation of assistance and evaluation, current thought is beginning to solidify around the notion of "the necessary relationship between assessment and support. Still, questions about the meaning of support and the function of assessment remain. Responsibility for summative assessment may come from outside assessors or may be handled by the same person responsible for assistance."[11]

Many of us in education have been uncomfortable with the idea of mixing the roles of *helper* and *evaluator* when it comes to new teachers. If we are truly interested in reprofessionalizing education, however, it may be time to take on this responsibility as our colleagues in medicine and law have done.

NOTES

1. Anne Newton et al., *Mentoring: A Resource and Training Guide for Educators* (Andover, MA: Regional Laboratory for Educational Improvement of the Northeast and Islands, 1994), 1.

2. Terry M. Wildman, Jerome A. Niles, Susan G. Magliaro, and Ruth Ann McLaughlin, "Teaching and Learning to Teach: The Two Roles of Beginning Teachers," *Elementary School Journal* 89, no. 4 (1989): 471–92.

3. Sharon Feiman-Nemser, "Teacher Mentoring: A Critical Review," 1996, Document #Ed397060, Sponsored by the Office of Educational Research and Improvement, Washington, DC.

4. Sharon Feiman-Nemser, Sharon Schwille, Cindy Carver, and Brian Yusko, *A Conceptual Review of Literature on New Teacher Induction* (E. Lansing, MI: National Partnership of Excellence and Accountability in Teaching [NPEAT], 1999), Document #Ed449147, Sponsored by the Office of Educational Research and Improvement, Washington, DC.

5. Feiman-Nemser, "Teacher Mentoring," 1.

6. Feiman-Nemser, "Teacher Mentoring"; Barry Sweeney, "Best Practice Resources," 2002. Available for download at http://www.teachermentors.com/.

7. Feiman-Nemser et al., *A Conceptual Review of Literature on New Teacher Induction*, 27.

8. *Education Week*, "Setting Policies for New Teachers," in *Editorial Projects in Education* 19, no. 18 (2002): 45–47, 48.

9. Mary T. Huber, "Disciplinary Styles in the Scholarship of Teaching: Reflections on the Carnegie Academy for the Scholarship of Teaching and Learning," *Disciplinary Styles in the Scholarship of Teaching and Learning: Exploring Common Ground* (Washington, DC: American Association for Higher Education, 2002), 27.

10. Ibid.

11. Feiman-Nemser et al., *A Conceptual Review of Literature on New Teacher Induction*, 27.

Mitchell Robinson is assistant professor of music education at Michigan State University.

The Mentor-Mentee Match: Preserving Tradition or Driving the Profession?

Mitchell Robinson

Traditionally, teaching has been a highly private act. It has been something done, for the most part, with the door closed. Many teachers, especially new teachers, are reluctant to share their problems or admit self-perceived weaknesses, believing them to be signs of weakness or incompetence and that "good teachers" work these problems out on their own. In fact, many teachers may limit their opportunities for interaction with colleagues in order to preserve their autonomy, one of the recognized benefits of teaching as a profession.

Compounding this scenario is the severe sense of isolation felt by many, if not most, music teachers, a feeling that is not limited to beginning music educators. This *individualistic orientation* to teaching[1] is one that is tacitly endorsed and reinforced by the school culture and by the practices of experienced teachers who often serve as the role models or mentor teachers for novices. Indeed, while some "mentor/novice pairs may create a sub-culture of inquiry and collaboration ... this may not be supported by the surrounding culture."[2] Breaking down these tacit barriers between *best practice* and the *status quo* should be a critical component of all good mentoring programs.

Mentoring can be a powerful means for passing on the traditions and techniques of a profession or can be used as a forum for critical reflection on one's practice in an effort to improve instruction and student learning. However, all mentors need comprehensive training in current "best practices" in order to advocate standards-based teaching among our newest colleagues, or the profession will not move forward.

The gap between current standards-based teaching and traditional methods and approaches has become much wider in the past decade or so, making it imperative that mentors are well versed in what is being taught in teacher preparation training courses, and, conversely, that collegiate faculty make sincere efforts to embed their students in authentic settings during these courses, preferably in collaboration with practicing music educators. State-sponsored and national beginning teacher assessments should also be clearly designed to drive the profession, rather than to merely reflect current practice, and these programs should be designed in tandem with teacher preparation standards at the appropriate music teacher preparation programs in the state or region.

PROGRAMS ACROSS THE COUNTRY

Effective mentoring is seen by most in the profession as the most important means for improving the induction and support of beginning teachers. Unfortunately, while more and more states are instituting new teacher induction and support programs—or reviving dormant programs—the picture nationwide is still not so encouraging. According to a 1999 survey conducted by *Education Week*,[3] twenty-eight states require or provide funds for districts to provide induction programs for novice teachers, but only nineteen states mandate that districts offer the programs to all beginning teachers; of those, only ten provide full or partial financial support.

The form and content of mentor training is also interpreted differently across the states. According to a fifty-state analysis of induction policies conducted by the American Federation of Teachers, twenty-nine states require that mentors be participants in the induction process, but only twenty-one of these states have established criteria for mentors. Many states offer only guidelines for mentors, such as successful teaching experience, strong appraisal ratings, and positive recommendations from principals and peers.[4]

While most of the states recognize the important role that mentors play in the induction process, their policies provide insufficient support for effective mentoring to take place. Although seventeen of the thirty-three states with state-mandated induction policies require that mentors receive training, only twelve of those states stipulate that mentors receive stipends—usually $500 to $1,000 per year.[5] Similarly, the gamut of mentor training models runs from the vague (Kansas: "a certified teacher who has completed three consecutive years of employment" and "exemplary teaching ability as demonstrated by criteria established by the state board") to the specific (Maine: mentors must receive "orientation and training ... in peer observation and assessment techniques").[6] The practice of states dictating unfunded mandates for local districts to implement without accompanying increases in revenues, a longtime public education policy ploy, appears to be alive and well in the new teacher induction arena.

Finally, only one other state besides Connecticut—New York—uses independent, compensated, state-trained assessors to evaluate beginning teachers. More common by far is the practice followed by thirty-one other states, where either individuals or teams from the new teacher's own school are required to conduct the evaluation process.[7] While the question of "assessment versus assistance" is still a hotly debated policy issue in the profession, it is ironic that the subject of new teacher induction and mentoring is widely viewed as a state-level policy issue, while the "dirty work" of actually evaluating new teacher effectiveness is left up to individual districts and schools, often with little or no guidance or assistance from the state.

MATCHMAKING

Care must be taken in mentor selection and mentor-mentee matching to assure that beginning teachers will be able to meet the standards that the profession is now agreeing upon for exemplary performance. Unfortunately, not every teacher who volunteers for the role of mentor is ideally suited for this kind of work. Some individuals perceive mentoring as a way out of the classroom or as a means of reducing their teaching loads or interactions with children—not valid criteria for becoming a mentor. Even more troubling are those experienced teachers who view mentoring as a forum for promoting "individual preference and personal style ... (over) shared standards of practice or ... a sense of collective responsibility for student learning."[8] In these cases, dyadic or one-on-one mentoring may actually "reinforce the ... privacy of teaching,"[9] subverting the power of mentoring to bring novices into the broader community of teachers and learners that can provide the support that all beginning teachers need.

This misinterpretation of the mentor-mentee relationship can be seen in the plethora of conference sessions with titles like "What They Didn't Teach You in Methods Class," or "Top 10 Tips for *Really* Surviving the First Year of Teaching." Although certainly well-intentioned, this spin on the mentoring process serves no purpose other than to frighten novice (and preservice) teachers and to reinforce their tacit beliefs that "learning to teach is basically something you do on your own with a little advice on the side."[10]

We also need to advocate as a profession for discipline-specific mentoring whenever possible. While our colleagues in general education believe that *building matches* are the most important criteria in matching beginning teachers with appropriate mentors, most researchers in music education[11] believe that the *content-area match* is a far more powerful and better predictor of success.

MENC's position statement on alternative certification addresses the issue of music-specific mentor matches by concluding that "professional development, supervision, and structured guidance should be delivered in a way that is consistent with reaching the teaching goals set out in the states' standards. This strongly implies, and MENC strongly recommends, that most of this mentoring must be delivered by individuals with acknowledged expertise in the field of study—most logically by colleagues. For prospective music teachers, this

135

means another music teacher who is experienced and acknowledged by peers as outstanding."[12]

There is a great deal of value in grouping new teachers in support cohorts, even across disciplines—"Beginning Teacher Buddies" (new teachers hired by the same school or district who form mutually supportive networks) were very important in my study of new music teachers in Connecticut. If there is no close BT Buddy, however, we need to encourage schools to think outside of the box when it comes to finding support for their new teachers. For example, districts should be empowered to look beyond their own borders to find appropriate mentors for their new teachers, trading or swapping matches across districts if funds are not transferrable between districts.

Other strategies include helping new teachers form their own groups or for colleges and universities to start new teacher networks in their areas. In Connecticut, the Connecticut Music Educators Association holds a new teacher reception at the state conference every year. This event has become an important means for helping new teachers connect to their professional organizations, to find other new music teachers in their region, and to set expectations for contin-ued growth and involvement in professional development activities during a crucial period in the beginning teachers' professional identity and role development.

It seems clear that the relationship between the beginning music teacher and the mentor—or mentors—can be among the most important factors in ensuring a smooth entry to the profession for the novice. It is critical, however, that care be taken in identifying, recruiting, and training potential mentors so that the knowledge transferred from expert to beginner not only preserves those tradi-tions worth carrying on to new generations, but also drives the profession forward. To accomplish both of these goals, mentors must be well-versed in cur-rent standards-based teaching strategies and techniques, aware of the unique needs of new teachers, and committed not only to the professional development of the novice, but also to their own continued growth as reflective educators.

NOTES

1. Sharon Feiman-Nemser, Sharon Schwille, Cindy Carver, and Brian Yusko, *A Conceptual Review of Literature on New Teacher Induction* (E. Lansing, MI: National Partnership of Excellence and Accountability in Teaching [NPEAT], 1999), Document #Ed449147, Sponsored by the Office of Educational Research and Improvement, Washington, DC.

2. Ibid., 20.

3. *Education Week*, "Setting Policies for New Teachers," *Editorial Projects in Education* 19, no. 18 (2000): 45–47, 48.

4. American Federation of Teachers, "Beginning Teacher Induction: The Essential Bridge," *Educational Issues Policy Brief,* no. 13 (2001), 5.

5. Ibid.

6. Ibid.

7. *Education Week*, "Setting Policies for New Teachers."

8. Feiman-Nemser et al., *A Conceptual Review of Literature on New Teacher Induction*, 29.

9. Ibid.

10. Ibid.

11. Colleen M. Conway, "Perceptions of Beginning Teachers, Mentors, and Administrators Regarding Preservice Music Teacher Preparation," *Journal of Research in Music Education* 50, no. 1 (2002): 20–36; Lisa DeLorenzo, "Perceived Problems of Beginning Music Teachers," *Bulletin of the Council for Research in Music Education,* no. 113 (1992): 9–25; Patti J. Krueger, "New Music Teachers Speak out on Mentoring," *Journal of Music Teacher Education* 8, no. 2 (1999): 7–13.

12. MENC, position paper on Alternative Certification, 2003. Available for download at http://www.menc.org/connect/surveys/Policy/altcertstatement.html.

Mitchell Robinson is assistant professor of music education at Michigan State University.

The Teacher Shortage Versus Alternative Routes to Certification

Mitchell Robinson

There is no question that we are currently in the midst of a serious teacher shortage, especially in particular areas of the country and in certain content and certification areas. It is currently estimated that between 20 and 50 percent of public school teachers leave their positions within three to seven years, and 9.3 percent quit before finishing their first year.[1] Further, Quaglia suggests that "the most qualified beginning teachers may be the first to leave."[2]

The number of students eighteen to twenty-one years of age, who have historically formed the recruitment base for traditional teacher preparation programs, is growing smaller, and fewer of these students are enrolling as teacher education majors. "Between 1975 and 1984 the proportion of college students majoring in education declined from 21 percent to 9 percent and the number of newly qualified teachers dropped by more than 50 percent—from 261,000 to 105,000."[3]

In music, the shortage appears most acute in our large cities and small rural districts, in strings and general music, and at the middle level. Many large suburban districts are actually benefiting from the higher degree of teacher mobility (perhaps due to the current shortage?) by attracting quality, veteran teachers when positions open and paying top scale and step for their experience. Conversely, positions in poor and urban districts are going unfilled, or programs are being cut, creating crisis conditions in places where music programs are already in peril. As the saying goes, "The rich get richer, while the poor get poorer."

At the same time, pressures are mounting from various stakeholders to increase the size of the teaching workforce by opening up teaching to people without professional preparation and granting them emergency or alternative certificates. These programs, referred to as "alternative routes to certification"

(ARC), have proliferated in recent years with the number of states allowing such programs doubling from eighteen in 1986 to forty in 1992.[4] In Connecticut, the Alternative Route to Certification (ARC) program now produces more music teachers than all of the state's university-based music teacher preparation programs combined.

Given the obvious tension between the current teacher shortage and the proliferation of ARC programs nationwide, we must ask ourselves, "Is ARC the answer?" As with any complex question, the answer is necessarily complicated: *yes, no,* and *maybe.*

BACKGROUND

First, a bit of historical context may be helpful. Alternate routes to certification for teachers are not new. The first teacher training and certification programs in the U.S. were not universities but school districts. In the nineteenth century, many large urban districts developed "normal schools" to train their own teachers for employment in local schools. These "normal schools" eventually became teachers colleges, but it was not until the early 1900s that teacher preparation became the responsibility of higher education.[5]

In modern times, the pressure to bypass traditional avenues of teacher preparation has come primarily from concerns that emerged during the early 1980s.[6] These concerns centered on the relationship between (allegedly) poorly prepared teachers and the failure of America's educational system to adequately prepare students to compete in the world marketplace. "On the basis of such findings, policy makers tended to blame teacher education programs for failing to recruit academically superior teachers."[7]

To this end, ARC programs were originally designed to target mid-career workers (i.e., thirty years of age and older) in other professions, typically business, engineering, and the military. These individuals were presumed to have "significant life experience" and superior content area knowledge, with at least a bachelor's degree in their chosen field, that would qualify them as expert teachers. The dream was to attract large numbers of dissatisfied or retired doctors, lawyers, scientists, and military personnel into the teaching workforce, providing an influx of much-needed talent, passion, and bodies.

ARC programs vary greatly nationwide in terms of purpose, content, and structure.[8] These programs also vary in terms of quality, often due to differing policy considerations. For example, ARC programs created to address severe, localized teacher shortages tend to focus on expediency and getting newly certified teachers into classrooms as quickly as possible. These programs often rely on transcript and resume analysis in order to grant certification and offer little or no actual course work or supervised teaching experience. In places where the improvement of teacher quality or the recruitment of a more diverse workforce is the goal, ARC candidates may be required to "complete the equivalency of a traditional approved program of teacher preparation."[9] ARC programs, therefore, tend to focus on the pragmatic aspects of teaching—what to do tomorrow and how to survive one's first year of teaching—more than the theoretical or philosophical aspects of teaching and learning.[10]

Current ARC programs, however, differ substantially from the above model in several key areas. Perhaps due to the pressures created by the teacher shortage, few ARC programs today adhere to strict age guidelines or degree requirements when accepting candidates. In many places, the typical ARC music applicant is a recent college graduate, twenty-two to twenty-five years of age, who holds a degree in music, fine arts, or a "related field," and who may or may not have some experience singing or playing an instrument. In other places, "any college graduate (or, as in Texas, anyone with 'some' college) can simply find a district to hire them."[11]

The "new" ARC programs are creating what is becoming in many places an "underclass" of teachers: a group of novice educators with little professional preparation who are often among the last hired and are offered the least desirable positions—those with challenging working conditions, difficult clienteles, few resources, low salaries, and poor administrative support. Further, researchers are discovering that teachers in some content areas (e.g., vocational education) who have been brought into the profession "through non-traditional routes have abnormally high turnover rates as compared to other ... teachers, indicating that alternate certification may not be effective as a recruitment device."[12]

Yes: THE CASE FOR ARC

If the teacher shortage is creating problems in schools across the country, then the situation in urban schools is in full-blown crisis mode. Throughout this century, "there has been a shortage of professionally educated teachers in the major urban areas no matter how many teachers were being prepared nationally."[13] In spite of widespread recognition of the problem, traditional teacher education programs have not done a good job of addressing this issue. The facts remain that the typical teacher education graduate is white, middle class, grew up in a suburban or rural area, and "prefers to teach in a suburban rather than urban school,"[14] while by the year 2020 about 40 percent of the K–12 population will be students of color.[15]

The requirements of traditional teacher education programs are seen by some as "barriers" that prevent qualified minority individuals from entering the profession.[16] As fewer minority students enter teaching, students of color are deprived of the kinds of positive role models that are so important to their growth, and our schools are deprived of the kind of diverse teaching force so crucial to the mission of a democratic and equitable education for all students.

141

It stands to reason that if a new population of candidates is to be recruited into teaching, then entry into the field will need to be made more flexible.

Alternative certification programs may be part of the answer in solving this problem. Studies of ARC programs in California, New Jersey, and Texas demonstrate that the population recruited into these programs differs markedly from the traditional teacher education population on several demographic dimensions.[17] Alternatively prepared teachers also tend to be older and are more likely to be minority males who have transferred from other occupations.

These teachers also have more experience living and working in urban environments and are more interested in working in the inner cities,[18] an important difference from most traditionally prepared teachers. Between 1986 and 1991, more than ten thousand new teachers were recruited through alternate routes in nine states in the southern U.S.,[19] while in 1989–90, Texas alone enrolled 1,064 new teachers in its alternative route program.[20] Between 1984 and 1990, the Los Angeles Unified School District recruited 1,100 new teachers through the alternate route program, many of these in the high need areas of math, science, and bilingual education.[21]

In some places, the alternative route to teacher certification is viewed as a primary means of attracting minority professionals into the classroom. In Texas, approximately 50 percent of ARC interns were from minority groups, and 30 percent were males; this compares to a Texas teaching force that is 22 percent minority and 22 percent male.[22] In Los Angeles, one third of the teachers recruited through ARC programs have been from minority groups. Alternative route candidates are also more likely than college-based teacher candidates to hold high expectations for low-income and minority students.[23]

This research indicates that alternate routes can be effective in recruiting a diverse group of individuals to teach in hard-to-staff schools, but does not tell us whether they stay in teaching or what kind of teachers they become. If these alternatively prepared teachers are to succeed—indeed, if they are to *survive*—then serious thought needs to be given to the form, content, and structure of ARC programs and to the kinds of follow-up professional development activities that should be designed for these teachers. To date, little research has been devoted to the professional development of alternatively prepared teachers. "Once again a radical reform is being rushed into place without thoughtful research and analysis."[24]

No: THE CASE AGAINST ARC

The move toward alternate routes represents a countervailing trend. Alternate certification programs move toward less professional education and toward the deregulation of teacher education. This move sets teaching apart from other professions—such as law, medicine, and psychology—where completion of an approved program of professional training from an accredited college is a mandatory prerequisite to professional licensing ... This movement associates teaching more with trades—such as carpentry, plumbing, electrical work— where on-the-job training in the form of apprenticeships is the norm. Despite this lack of information, alternate routes into teaching are proliferating. Two thirds of the states have already dispensed with the approved program requirement as a prerequisite for professional licensing for teachers; several others have legislation pending.[25]

How one feels about alternate teacher certification often depends on the assumptions that one holds about teaching. In music teacher education, many believe that educators benefit from the *simultaneous* accumulation of knowledge about content and pedagogy and that this learning is best accomplished over an extended period of time. These teacher educators are designing methods courses and field experiences that provide their students with rich, contextual interactions with school-age students in authentic settings, often referred to as *Professional Development Sites* or *Partnerships*.[26]

Proponents of alternate route programs, on the other hand, believe that teachers do not need university-based professional training in teaching. They believe that teachers develop the ability to teach in relatively simple ways— "through knowing their subject, through learning to teach on the job, or by being a 'natural teacher'"[27]—and that much educational course work, such as methods and educational foundations classes, is simply a waste of time.

However, an examination of some of the common assumptions about teaching that have fueled the drive towards alternate certification initiatives reveal troubling inconsistencies when compared to the research literature. For example, there is a strongly held belief by many ARC supporters that if one knows a subject well, one is qualified to teach it. While it is difficult to argue with the premise that in order to teach effectively teachers should be competent in their subject area, research efforts to show a relationship between teacher content knowledge and teacher effectiveness have been largely inconclusive.[28] In fact, teacher candidates with extensive course work in their content area often still have difficulty explaining basic concepts, and few can give comprehensible explanations or examples of basic principles and meanings.[29]

Other research in cognitive psychology suggests that advanced knowledge of subject matter

> may actually impede effective communication of concepts. As individuals develop expertise in a subject, they develop a "technical shorthand" ... that is not easily understood by novices. Effective teaching requires the expert to unpack, expand, and simplify his personal knowledge. Such pedagogical

> understandings are not typically acquired with subject matter expertise but need to be developed and viewed as distinct professional knowledge and skills.[30]

In other words, personal knowledge of music may not be equivalent to being able to teach music.

There is also an assumption among ARC proponents that learning to teach is best accomplished "on the job." This assumption holds that teaching is a "pragmatic art," that some people are "born teachers," and that anyone with a bachelor's degree and some basic background in the subject matter to be taught can become competent through on-the-job training. Recent research with teachers who "learn on the job," however, has shown that novice teachers, without proper guidance and support, "often learn lessons ... that restrict their ability to explore a variety of instructional practices and undermine teachers' ability to continue to learn from experience over a career."[31]

In another study, university-educated teachers were introduced to ideas about cutting-edge theories and "best practices" in their fields, while alternate route teachers (who were prepared more *locally* than *globally*) tended to develop "restricted and highly idiosyncratic approaches to instruction ... based on their own learning, and life and work experiences."[32] While personal experiences and talents should be a valued part of any teacher's instructional tool kit, the ARC teachers in this case were developing a modal, or unidimensional, approach to instruction that was then "applied and misapplied, with little opportunity to reflect on and critically analyze the consequence of their teaching actions."[33]

Many localized ARC initiatives, for example, are taught solely or primarily by local teachers and focus on implementing district curricula, understanding school system policies and procedures, and negotiating the "system." By relying solely on localized preparation for teaching, ARC programs may be inadvertently narrowing the range of settings for which their teachers are prepared. Although these teachers are often granted broad certification in a specific content area (K–12 certification, for example, is common in music), it is possible that the limited preparation offered in many ARC programs will serve to restrict these teachers' ability to function effectively in the global range of teaching settings for which their certification allows. These teachers, in effect, become *one trick ponies*, unable to meet the demands of challenging and changing classroom settings and conditions.

Finally, as mentioned above, research indicates that many ARC programs report troublingly high rates of teacher turnover.[34] Although traditional teacher education programs are also plagued by poor retention rates, this finding has the potential to negate what for some has been the most tantalizing promise of ARC initiatives: the recruitment—and retention—of a more diverse teaching force for today's schools.

Maybe: SUGGESTIONS, CRITIQUES, SOLUTIONS

> Both traditional and alternate routes to teacher preparation need improvement. The current crop of alternate routes do not seem to significantly improve teacher learning, but they also may be no worse than many college-based programs. To achieve new goals for increased subject matter understanding for all students, teachers will need to learn much that they have not previously been asked to know—about the subjects and students they teach, about the connections between schools and other parts of society, and about teachers' own learning. The improvement of teacher preparation will probably require closer work between school sites and colleges, without giving up what either has to offer.[35]

Clearly, we need to consider the long-term effects of adding large numbers of alternatively prepared teachers to the workforce during a time of shortage. These teachers often require more mentoring and supervision, and they work in the most challenging placements available—and with the least amount of professional preparation for these conditions. If ARC is to deliver on its promise to expand and diversify the teacher workforce, then serious thought and discussion need to be devoted to the following issues:

• ARC music initiatives should become more focused on recruiting and preparing teachers for those positions that historically have been the most difficult to fill: jobs in urban schools, string music positions, and positions at the middle level, to name just a few. With a vision focused more clearly on these areas of need, ARC organizers and instructors may be better able to design instructional programs targeted on the unique challenges and issues inherent to these specific teaching assignments.

• If improving the diversity of the teaching force is an important goal of ARC initiatives, then we should put additional financial resources into supporting and retaining candidates in high-need areas such as those mentioned above and into attracting and nurturing minority teachers across teaching levels and assignments. We have a historic opportunity in the years ahead not only to replace the music teachers leaving the classroom but also to ensure that the teachers of the future more accurately reflect the society and culture of the students whom they will be teaching. To not seize this opportunity would be a dereliction of our duty as stewards of the profession.

• It seems inequitable, if not patently unfair, for ARC teachers (some of whom spend as few as three weeks in training and have no formal music teaching practice prior to entering the classroom) and traditionally prepared teachers (many of whom have spent as many as five or six years in college studying and practicing before entering the field) to be granted identical forms of certification upon completion of their training program. The "No Child Left Behind" (NCLB) Act of 2001 appears to recognize this inequity by requiring that "teachers hired through alternative certification must ... assume functions as a teacher only for a specified period of time not to exceed three years."[36]

In order to rectify this inequity in certification granting, perhaps alternate certification should be *delimited* in terms of time, range of assignment, or both. For example, an applied violin major might be approved for a three-year period to teach string lessons and orchestra class, but not general music, chorus, or any other music class; similarly, a vocal music major or church choir director might be authorized to teach chorus and voice lessons for a period of three years, but not instrumental music.

Under this form of delimited certification, alternatively prepared teachers would be approved for a specified period of time to teach classes in their specific area of expertise and background but would be disallowed from teaching music classes that would fall outside of the candidates' area of expertise. More accurate matching of candidates' skills with their teaching assignments should have the multiple benefits of improving teacher retention rates while also increasing teacher effectiveness. All ARC teachers who successfully complete this initial delimited period of service should be encouraged to become fully certified by pursuing an appropriate graduate degree in music education at an accredited institution of higher education.

• In order to provide more entry points into teaching for those with bachelor's degrees in music, we should encourage the creation of more "master's degree with teacher certification" programs. These programs fill an important niche in the current array of degree offerings in music education but are not plentiful enough in all areas of the country to meet the needs of all who want to enter the teaching force. Existing "master's with certification" programs should be enlarged and strengthened, and start-up funds should be made available for the development of new programs, especially in areas that are currently poorly serviced.

• Many of the criticisms of existing college-based teacher preparation programs contain undeniable elements of accuracy. Some course work in education is not as rigorous as it should be, and what is taught in methods classes is often unconnected to current practice or not informed by the best of our research knowledge about the teaching and learning process. Efforts at improving undergraduate teacher preparation programs might begin by focusing on improving the quality of "field experiences" provided to music education students and by strengthening the connections between collegiate and PreK–12 music educators and programs.[37] There is much promise in the notion of *Professional Development Sites* and *Partnerships*,[38] an idea borrowed from our colleagues in general education that is just beginning to gain a foothold in music education circles.

● To address criticisms of a university monopoly in teacher education, resources should be devoted to "incubators" of fresh, new approaches to teacher certification. These new delivery systems for licensure (which might include state departments of education, state music education associations, teachers' associations, and local districts' professional development operations) should be held to the same accountability standards as higher education. Praxis and state teacher assessment scores should be tracked and analyzed by training agencies, with rewards granted to those whose graduates do well and sanctions put in place against those agencies whose graduates do not prove effective in the classroom.

With more new teachers coming into the profession through nontraditional routes, the process of beginning teacher induction and evaluation becomes, in many ways, our last, best chance to effect positive change in a systemic manner and give our newest colleagues in the profession their best chance to succeed. We owe them—and our students—no less.

NOTES

1. Barry Sweeney, "Best Practice Resources," 2002. Available for download at http://www.teachermentors.com/; Phillip Schlechty and Victor S. Vance, "Recruitment, Selection, and Retention: The Shape of the Teaching Force," *Elementary School Journal* 83, no. 4 (1983): 469–87.

2. Russ Quaglia, "Socialization of the Beginning Teacher: A Theoretical Model from the Empirical Literature," *Research in Rural Education* 53 (1989): 1–7.

3. N. B. Carey, B. S. Mittman, and Linda Darling-Hammond, *Recruiting Mathematics and Science Teachers Through Non-traditional Programs* (Santa Monica, CA: Rand Corporation, 1988); National Center for Education Statistics, *Digest of Education Statistics* (Washington, DC: U.S. Department of Education, 1987); National Center for Education Statistics, *New Teachers in the Market, 1987* update (Washington, DC: U.S. Department of Education, 1990).

4. C. Emily Feistritzer, "National Overview of Alternative Certification," *Education and Urban Society* 26, no. 1 (1993): 18–28.

5. M. Haberman, "Alternative Teacher Certification Programs," *Action in Teacher Education* 8, no. 2 (1986): 13–18; F. W. Lutz and J. B. Hutton, "Alternative Teacher Certification: Its Policy Implications for Classroom and Personnel Practice,"*Educational Evaluation and Policy Analysis* 11, no. 3 (1989): 237–54.

6. National Commission on Excellence in Education, *A Nation at Risk* (Washington, DC: U.S. Government Printing Office, 1983).

7. Trish Stoddart and Robert E. Floden, "Traditional and Alternative Routes to Teacher Certification: Issues, Assumptions, and Misconceptions," Issue Paper 95–2, National Center for Research on Teacher Learning, Michigan State University, 1995, p. 5. Available for download at http://ncrtl.msu.edu/http/ipapers/html/ip952.htm.

8. Linda Darling-Hammond, "Teaching and Knowledge: Policy Issues Posed by Alternate Certification for Teachers," *Peabody Journal of Education* 67, no. 3 (1992): 123–54.

9. Stoddart and Floden, "Traditional and Alternative Routes to Teacher Certification," 8.

10. Trish Stoddart and Robert E. Floden, "School District-Based Teacher Training: An Alternative Route to Teacher Certification" (paper presented at the annual meeting of the American Educational Research Association, San Francisco, 1989).

11. Stoddart and Floden, "Traditional and Alternative Routes to Teacher Certification," 2.

12. Ibid., 3.

13. Haberman, "Alternative Teacher Certification Programs."

14. Feistritzer, "National Overview of Alternative Certification."

15. A. Pallas, G. Natriello, and E. McDill, "The Changing Nature of the Disadvantaged Population," *Educational Researcher,* no. 185 (1989): 16–22.

16. J. Alter, P. Wingert, and A. McDaniel, "A Summit for Schools," *Newsweek* CXIV, no. 56 (October 2, 1989): 58.

17. W. R. Houston, F. Marshall, and T. McDavid, "Problems of Traditionally Prepared and Alternatively Certified First-Year Teachers," *Education and Urban Society* 26, no. 1 (1993): 78–89; G. Natriello and Karen Zumwalt, "New Teachers for Urban Schools? The Contribution of the Provisional Teacher Program in New Jersey," *Education and Urban Society* 26, no. 1 (1993): 49–62; Trish Stoddart, "The Los Angeles Unified School District Intern Program: Recruiting and Preparing Teachers for an Urban Context," *Peabody Journal of Education* 67, no. 3 (1992): 84–122.

18. Stoddart, "The Los Angeles Unified School District Intern Program"; Feistritzer, "National Overview of Alternative Certification."

19. W. Corbin, *Facts and Figures for South Carolina's Critical Needs Certification Program* (Rock Hill, SC: Winthrop College, 1991).

20. Texas Education Agency, *Alternative Teacher Certification in Texas* (Austin, TX: Author, 1990).

21. Stoddart, "The Los Angeles Unified School District Intern Program."

22. Texas Education Agency, *Alternative Teacher Certification in Texas.*

23. Stoddart, "The Los Angeles Unified School District Intern Program."

24. Stoddart and Floden, "Traditional and Alternative Routes to Teacher Certification," 9.

25. Feistritzer, "National Overview of Alternative Certification," quoted in Stoddart and Floden, "Traditional and Alternative Routes to Teacher Certification."

26. Susan W. Conkling and W. Henry, "Professional Development Partnerships: A New Model for Music Teacher Preparation," *Arts Education Policy Review* 100, no. 4 (1999): 19–23; Mitchell Robinson, "From Visitors to Partners: The Evolution of a Methods Course," *Journal of Music Teacher Education* 11, no. 1 (2001): 21–26.

27. Stoddart and Floden, "Traditional and Alternative Routes to Teacher Certification," 3.

28. D. L. Ball, "Knowledge and Researching in Mathematical Pedagogy: Examining What Prospective Teachers Bring to Teacher Education" (Ph.D. diss., Michigan State University, East Lansing, 1988); D. L. Ball, "Unlearning to Teach Mathematics," *For the Learning of Mathematics* 8, no. 1 (1988): 40–48.

29. Ball, "Knowledge and Researching in Mathematical Pedagogy."

30. M. T. Chi, R. Glaser, and E. Rees, "Expertise in Problem Solving," in *Advances in the Psychology of Human Intelligence* (Hillsdale, NJ: Erlbaum, 1982), 7–75, quoted in Stoddart and Floden, "Traditional and Alternative Routes to Teacher Certification," 10.

31. Sharon Feiman-Nemser and M. Buchmann, "When Is Student Teaching Teacher Education?" *Teacher and Teacher Education* 3 (1987): 255–73; J. Hoffman and S. Edwards,

eds., *Clinical Teacher Education: Reform and Reality* (Austin: University of Texas, 1986).

32. Mary Louise Gomez and T. Stoddart, "Learning to Teach Writing: The Balancing of Personal and Professional Perspectives," in *Focal Points: Qualitative Inquiries into Teaching* (Washington, DC: American Educational Research Association, 1991).

33. Trish Stoddart, "Learning to Teach English, Mathematics, and Science in an Alternative Route to Teacher Certification," *The Curriculum Journal* 2, no. 3 (1991): 259–81.

34. J. Lee, *Programs for Training Vocational Teachers in Selected Areas of Teacher Shortage* (Mississippi State University: Mississippi State Department of Agricultural Extension Education, 1978), Eric Document Reproduction Service No. Ed 226217; L. Nasman, "Here's How to Fill Those Vocational Education Slots," *American School Board Journal* 66, no. 3 (1979): 42–43.

35. Stoddart and Floden, "Traditional and Alternative Routes to Teacher Certification," 14.

36. MENC, position paper on Alternative Certification, 2003. Available for download at http://www.menc.org/connect/surveys/Policy/altcertstatement.html.

37. Mitchell Robinson, "A Theory of Collaborative Music Education between Higher Education and Urban Public Schools" (Ph.D. diss., University of Rochester, Eastman School of Music, Rochester, NY, 1999).

38. Conkling and Henry, "Professional Development Partnerships"; Robinson, "From Visitors to Partners."

Mitchell Robinson is assistant professor of music education at Michigan State University.

Ongoing Professional Development

Colleen M. Conway

Each year that I teach strengthens me for the next year and gives me more experience from which to draw. I was going to use the clichéd analogy that becoming a great teacher is like a fine wine or cheese that grows more rich over time, but that development is passive and not necessarily dependent on an active relationship with its environment. I'd rather use a less refined but more accurate analogy drawn from my experience of playing the harp. Becoming a better teacher is like a harpist developing the calluses on the tips of her fingers. It is a gradual process and is often painful in the beginning. The layers of toughness are built one by one and through the experience of continued learning, practice, and performance. There may also be times when your finger seems to shed itself completely of its layers, only to begin the building process again. The result for the harpist, as well as for the developing teacher, is a protective and supportive layer created through consistent and continuing lessons with a caring teacher, interactions with other musicians and with the audience, hours of dedication to practice and performance, and an intense belief that every good and bad experience adds to the strength of the callus. Successful beginning teachers understand that they may not be in control of what happens to them on their journey to become a better teacher, but they are in control of how they react to what happens to them, and they are in control of their choice to learn and grow from each positive and negative experience. This year, I was told by a fellow teacher that one interpretation of the word "chaos" is "opportunity." For your first years of teaching and beyond, success is the ability to find positive opportunity in everything. (Jill Wozniak-Reese, elementary music teacher)

As I have interviewed beginning and experienced teachers, I have found across the board that teachers who have views similar to the ones expressed above by Jill Wozniak-Reese are the ones who stay in the profession and are most successful. Expert teachers view each year with a new energy and excitement and each class and each student as a new learning opportunity. Quality professional development can help the music teacher capture this energy and excitement year after year. Michael Smith and Paul Haack suggest:

> More than ever before, thorough preparation and continuous, ongoing development of teachers is being viewed as the best way to improve schools. Teachers do make a difference, teacher education makes a difference, and continuing professional development makes a difference. All music educators need places where they can be refreshed and renewed. We need lifelong rejuvenation if we are to continue to remain professionally healthy and personally satisfied.[1]

Professional development for music educators that is sponsored by music organizations seeks to support music teachers.[2] However, the research base concerning the professional development experiences of music teachers is quite small.[3] It is sometimes difficult for professional development organizers to base decisions about programs on research evidence of music teachers' needs. Mary Hookey outlines an agenda for research on professional development and asks: "What are the purposes and consequences of professional development experiences, and in what ways are the teachers individually or collectively implicated in their professional development?"[4] My response in this chapter to Hookey's inquiry is based on e-mail questionnaire responses, individual interviews, and phone interviews from a diverse group of more than forty music teachers (choral, band, string, and elementary general) at various points in their careers (beginning teachers through retired teachers) about their perceptions of professional development in music education. Research questions included (a) What are the most challenging aspects of your job?, (b) What types of professional development support have been most useful to you?, and (c) What are the rewards of your work?

Based on an analysis of the written and interview responses, the Emerging as a Teacher sidebar includes (a) challenges to music teachers that seem to get easier as the teachers become more experienced and (b) challenges that continue throughout one's career as a music educator. In coding these challenges, I used some of the categories of beginning teacher

---

EMERGING AS A TEACHER

What Gets Easier?

- Security and self-confidence
- Classroom management
- Administrative organization (preparing a budget, etc.)
- Lesson planning (timing of lessons, understanding grade-level expectations)
- Finding materials and resources for lessons
- Community relations/parent interactions

Career-long Challenges

- Time management
- Advocacy for music (communicating the value of music education to colleagues or administration)
- Isolation (left out of decision making)
- Curriculum concerns (choosing literature and classroom activities)
- Scheduling
- Keeping up with educational trends
- Finding time for own musical growth

concerns developed by Lisa DeLorenzo[5] and Patti Krueger[6] that were discussed in depth in Paul Haack's chapter.

Several years ago I took some data from my beginning music teacher study in mid-Michigan to Sharon Feiman-Nemser, who is one of the foremost authorities on beginning teacher research. As she was helping me make sense of the data I had from beginning music teachers, one of her comments to me was: "I wonder if what you are studying is as much the culture of the workplace of a music teacher as it is an examination of issues facing beginning teachers." As I compared the issues from DeLorenzo's and Krueger's work with the responses from more experienced teachers, I began to agree with Feiman-Nemser that many issues that are problematic for beginning music teachers remain as challenges for music teachers throughout their careers.

WHAT TYPES OF PROFESSIONAL DEVELOPMENT SUPPORT ARE HELPFUL

> At present, while professional development is dictated by state and/or local education agencies and recognized as necessary by educators themselves, such development is generally not supported, either with funding or by releasing teachers from their teaching responsibilities. Regardless of the global recognition of the importance of continuing education, it frequently remains the responsibility of educators to obtain and finance their own professional development. Therefore, educators with professional development requirements, both imposed by outside agencies and for personal growth, must consider opportunities that are affordable, do not conflict with their daily teaching schedule, and meet their needs in terms of licensure, employment retainment, advancement, curricular demands, and personal teaching skills development. Teachers continue to seek short-term, affordable, quality experiences, generally in the form of workshops.[7]

As Chelcy Bowles suggests above, professional development specific to music is not often offered within schools themselves. Music teachers must find many of these experiences on their own. All of the teachers I spoke with about professional development were sure to mention that professional development within music was the most helpful. For example, a high school choral teacher said, "Going to *music* conferences was the most helpful thing. I have the opportunity to listen and observe great ensembles and go to workshops that are directly related to what I do every day. However, it is sometimes difficult to persuade the district to allow my attendance at these conferences, as opposed to seminars on brain-based learning, reading readiness, or state tests." As has been mentioned previously with regard to beginning music teacher induction and mentor policy, one of the most important things music administrators in policy positions can do is to help music teachers get permission to attend music-specific in-service workshops for professional development credit.

MUSIC TEACHER VIEWS OF PROFESSIONAL DEVELOPMENT

Chelcy Bowles conducted a survey of music teachers about their self-expressed professional development needs.[8] Although only 29.6 percent of the teachers who received the survey returned it, she did have 456 responses representing all grade levels and music teaching specialties (general, vocal, and instrumental). These respondents may not represent the views of all music teachers; however, the study did provide useful information for professional development designers to consider.

The most frequently chosen professional development topic areas chosen by her respondents were

- technology
- assessment
- choral/instrumental literature
- standards
- creativity
- grant writing

Other topics that were added by respondents in the "other" category on her survey tool included

- community relations/support/advocacy
- advanced vocal and instrumental pedagogy
- writing curriculum
- specific methodologies (Orff, Kodály, Dalcroze, CMP)
- brain research
- scheduling
- composition
- instrument repair
- multiage curriculum
- teacher training supervision

Respondents in Bowles's study suggested that university continuing education programs in the summers and national/state/local music organization conferences were their most preferred types of professional development venues. Her study also presents information on how far teachers are willing to travel for workshops (no more than one hundred miles), what they are willing to pay (no more than two hundred dollars a day), what type of housing is preferred (hotels), and how workshops should be scheduled (consecutive days in the summer and long weekends during the year).

INFORMAL INTERACTIONS AS PROFESSIONAL DEVELOPMENT

Many teachers in my study commented that the informal interactions they have with other music teachers are the most powerful sources of professional development support.

> Professional development for me now is the same as it's always been—trusted advice of colleagues whom I admire. The most I tend to get out of any conference is the collaboration with colleagues and bringing home a "morsel" of information that helps in some small way—whether it be a new work, a new way of doing something I've been doing for a long time, or whatever—the conversation with colleagues is and always has been the most helpful professional development. (High school instrumental music teacher)

> Without a doubt, the most meaningful professional development that I have had has been help in finding and developing classroom activities that foster musical growth in my students. In fact, I've found my school district's professional development days such a disappointment that I have had to go outside of the district to find a "planning mentor" specifically for the purpose of learning how to create my lesson plans more effectively. (Elementary general music teacher)

Michel Smith and Paul Haack encourage teachers to seek these informal experiences and suggest: "Music educators travel the road of lifelong development alone at their own risk. While an individual may feel just fine at times, it seems unwise to ignore the help that other professionals can provide in terms of different perspectives, realistic attitudes, good counsel, caring, and sharing."[9]

TEACHER ATTITUDE AND GENERAL IN-SERVICE PROGRAMS

There are some programs in the school that teachers must attend. In fact, in considering relationships with other nonmusic colleagues, it is crucial for music teachers to participate in some of the district-level professional development experiences. Several respondents to my inquiry discussed having a positive attitude about participation in generic workshops.

> In the general professional development workshops I have attended, I have found some parts useful, some not. I feel the best way to approach this kind of learning situation is to go in with the understanding that I may not be able to use all of it, but the attitude that I will try to get everything possible out of the experience. For example, there was a lot of emphasis on "best practices" procedures, some of which are not applicable to all aspects of music learning.

155

I've learned to pick and choose from what is offered at most district professional development activities. (Middle school instrumental music teacher)

PROFESSIONAL DEVELOPMENT INITIATIVES WITHIN MENC AND THE PROFESSION AT LARGE

Based on their analysis of professional development offerings at the 2000 National MENC Conference, Harry Price and Evelyn Orman suggested, "If contents of national conferences are intended to reflect the interests, directions, and concerns of those affiliated with a professional organization, it would be worthwhile to systematically query MENC members to examine how conference offerings ... and their trends adequately and accurately reflect the needs of those involved with teaching music and preparing music educators."[10]

Recognizing this ongoing need for responding to member interests and concerns, MENC has surveyed participants following recent national and division conferences. The survey results have given MENC guidance on programs for upcoming national conferences, as well as direction for other professional development programs. Also, MENC has begun to offer new session categories on the calls for proposals for these conferences.[11]

NATIONAL BOARD FOR PROFESSIONAL TEACHING STANDARDS

Another source of professional development now available to K–12 music teachers is the National Board for Professional Teaching Standards (NBPTS) certification process. This certification is available to licensed teachers on a voluntary basis. Qualifying teachers must pass performance-based assessments developed by NBPTS and teachers in the discipline. The assessments measure teaching practice against standards describing what accomplished music teachers should know and be able to do.[12] NBPTS first offered certification for music teachers in 2002.

Applying for National Board certification is an intensive process that offers teachers a unique professional development opportunity. According to NBPTS, "teachers report that they benefit immensely from the support of a facilitator, or candidate support provider, during the certification process."[13] This support may include "providing resources, mentoring, coaching, guidance, and technical assistance to candidates."[14] NBPTS provides information and guidance for facilitators, who may be accomplished teachers, staff developers, or higher education faculty. On a national level, these facilitators are not required to be NBPTS-certified. Certain school districts or states that offer stipends to these mentors may, however, have their own requirements.

The National Board has established relationships with numerous colleges and universities, some of which have created new courses—sometimes in conjunction with a master's program—for teachers seeking certification. Some higher education institutions conduct research on the impact of National Board certification on teachers, students, public policies, and education reform. With music teachers now eligible for certification, music researchers may wish to conduct related studies.[15]

National Board Certified Teachers (NBCTs) work to promote accomplished teaching in various ways. Some serve as mentors to new teachers, instructional leaders, curriculum developers, or adjunct faculty in colleges of education. Others provide support for NBPTS candidates. After completing intensive training sessions, some serve as assessors for candidate responses. Accomplished teachers who are not NBPTS-certified may also qualify to be assessors.

As of May 2003, 49 states and 486 local school districts, including the District of Columbia, have initiated legislative and policy action to provide incentives and recognition for NBCTs.[16] Incentives may include application fee support, salary supplements, license portability, license renewal, or continuing education units. The wide variety of professional development opportunities, support, and incentives available to music teachers are described on the NBPTS Web site at www.nbpts.org.

PROFESSIONAL DEVELOPMENT PROGRAMS: PLANNING FOR CAREER GROWTH[17]

Music educators must initiate career planning that guides professional growth and results in increased professional effectiveness and satisfaction. To achieve these results, music teachers must be prepared to make changes in their professional lives. Structured professional planning provides the necessary avenue through which inexperienced music educators can continue the growth process that began in the teacher certification program. In this regard, a professional development program is viewed as an aid to the induction of young teachers into the profession. The process for continued growth and professional advancement is linked to the support provided by an ever-expanding partnership of advisors.

Planning for professional growth as a music educator should begin prior to initial certification through discussions, seminars, and personal discussions with members of the partnership team. The newly certified music educator should formulate a Professional Development Plan by drawing on information from school personnel and by retaining the assistance of college advisors. Experienced professionals who have not yet entered into such a systematic process also should find the development of such a plan a supportive and positive experience.

The Professional Development Plan should take into account two major factors: (1) general professional development, to add depth and breadth to the music educator's knowledge, skills, and attitudes, and (2) individualized professional development, to provide specific opportunities for personal growth and professional advancement. General development primarily focuses on the quality of service to the employing institution, while individualized development centers on the quality of the teacher's career. Planning for general and individualized growth should be done in an organized and programmatic fashion.

The general aspect of professional development is meant to help teachers move beyond beginning competence. This factor accounts for the knowledge, skills, and understandings desired in a mature professional that were not addressed or developed fully in the teacher certification program. It suggests that the beginning teacher identify priority areas needing development by evaluating (1) the nature of the certification program, (2) academic performance, (3) student-teaching performance, and (4) the results of any professional qualifying examinations. (While the initial evaluations would be made with the partnership team that was formed for the professional induction period, later evaluations would ideally come from an extended partnership that includes colleagues, students, parents, school administrative staff, and college professors.)

The individualized aspect considers unique personal needs and differences by recognizing that professional growth, advancement, and continued interest in the profession generally require the establishment of personal long-term goals and assistance systems for growth and development. Developing expertise in special areas of interest, planning for career advancement within and beyond the current teaching area, and attaining personal rewards and satisfaction are fundamental to retaining excellent teachers in music education.

Professional Development Plans should be designed, therefore, to provide a formal and systematic process for the lifelong growth and advancement of music educators. While advanced academic study should be an integral part of a growth plan, various other experiences are worthwhile for music teachers, and such noncredit activities should be integrated into the professional development plan. Each music educator, however, should take the responsibility of initiating the process of forming the advisory group to assist with diagnoses for growth and prescriptions for change. During the early stages of a career, data relating to general and individualized development should be gathered on a semester or yearly basis. In later stages of a career, two- to three-year intervals may be sufficient. These personal assessments should be based on prior goals and point to new prescriptions for further growth as the time and resources needed for change are considered. Clearly, this process should be regarded as diagnostic and prescriptive rather than judgmental in order to provide an atmosphere that supports constructive self-criticism and helpful peer evaluation. The use of the information generated by this process should be determined by the individual. Such evaluation is envisioned to be the basis for personal planning, rewards, and recognition. An effective professional development program can:

For the Individual Music Educator

- provide professional growth and instructional improvement through objective evaluation and prescriptions for change
- enhance self-image and status in the profession
- contribute to professional satisfaction and professional advancement
- provide the impetus for making personal decisions about career outcomes throughout a professional lifetime

For the Music Education Profession

- develop close and continuing relationships between teachers at elementary/secondary schools and colleges
- involve professional organizations in the career development of music educators
- strengthen the communication and interaction among agencies that influence and affect music education
- account for an expanding and evolving professional responsibility in music education for the future

General Professional Development

Music educators need to become mature persons and professionals whose ongoing development allows them to meet responsibilities effectively and creatively. Attention needs to be given to expanding the depth and breadth of knowledge, to demands of increased competence, and to newly developed instructional methods and technology systems. Personal areas of greater and lesser strength and institutional needs become important in developing priorities among basic competence areas that include, but are not limited to, the following:

Personal

- becoming an increasingly independent, intrinsically motivated, and growth-oriented individual
- continuing to develop tolerance for and understanding of persons with different values, abilities, and backgrounds
- developing general communication and interpersonal skills
- continuing to develop and exemplify a mature code of conduct relating to appropriate ethical and moral expectations of the profession
- gaining the ability to accept personal and professional assessments of others and to assess oneself objectively
- gaining skills in managing funds and, when necessary, soliciting funds to enhance the regular curriculum

- participating in and contributing service to appropriate professional music and music education organizations, agencies, and boards
- assisting local school leadership in developing educational policies affecting music education and the schools in general
- becoming knowledgeable about local policies and state mandates affecting music programs and education
- extending personal leadership competencies
- gaining competence in maintaining records and professional correspondence
- gaining competence in problem solving relating to personnel, economic, and scheduling matters
- continuing to develop positive and supportive professional relationships with peers and students
- continuing to develop the sensitivity, empathy, and mature affective qualities that enhance all forms of human interaction

Intellectual

- cultivating curiosity in all aspects of music and education
- continuing to pursue new directions of learning in the various areas of the liberal arts and sciences
- developing the ability to assimilate information from new areas of study to enhance personal development and professional effectiveness
- applying creative-thinking skills and innovative ideas to all levels of the teaching/learning process
- keeping abreast of research pertaining to music, education, and related areas
- maintaining a researcher's attitude toward all aspects of instruction and evaluation
- developing the ability to communicate about professional matters across subject areas
- assessing public opinion of schooling in order to react responsibly as a professional leader

Musical

- furthering knowledge of theory, musicology, and ethnomusicology
- becoming familiar with current forms of technology regarding the creation, performance, reproduction, appreciation, uses, and abuses of music
- pursuing advanced study of pedagogy to increase understanding and mastery of music repertoire, teaching techniques, interpretation, and performance in major and secondary areas

- learning to arrange and compose music in a variety of forms and styles for a variety of purposes
- improvising instrumentally or vocally
- extending knowledge and understanding of psycho-acoustics and the influence of music on human behavior
- extending knowledge and understanding of the sociology of music and the uses and functions of music in America and other cultures and subcultures
- renewing personal musicianship and performance

Instructional

- developing a mature philosophy to serve as a foundation for teaching
- learning to teach to the appropriate level for all students, including special learners
- developing qualifications for adjunct teaching experiences in community or college settings
- contributing to curriculum assessments and evaluations
- relating music to other arts and to other areas of the curriculum
- understanding and relating the uses of music to effective daily living and positive human behavior
- increasing competence in developing short-term and long-term teaching plans
- learning to design effective courses and related teaching materials for a variety of student needs
- enhancing the ability to communicate musical content effectively using verbal and nonverbal methods
- expanding competencies in applying effective discipline and classroom management techniques
- becoming increasingly effective in selecting musical materials appropriate to various instructional settings and the varying needs of learners
- becoming increasingly familiar with repertoire for students at all grade levels
- enhancing knowledge of keyboard, fretted, and classroom instruments for purposes of demonstration and accompaniment
- becoming able to work effectively in an increasing variety of traditional and novel teaching situations
- gaining competence to serve as an advisor or supervisor of student teachers and interns

Individualized Professional Development

Practicing music educators need to monitor changes in their professional interests and aspirations continuously. As experience accumulates, a reevalua-

161

tion of personal potential and individual abilities may lead to professional advancement requiring increased specialization or new skills. One individual may become a master teacher with responsibilities in testing and measurement, curriculum design, or content-related resources. Another may move from classroom teaching to a supervisory or administrative position. Some teachers may find professional advancement by moving to a career that is related to music education but outside of teaching. Individualized development should contribute to personal effectiveness and advancement as well as provide for career satisfaction and a stronger and more effective profession of music educators.

Personal career advancement may be enhanced by, but not be limited to, the following options:

Personal

- leadership roles in music and art administration at the local, state, or national level
- administrative certification (supervisor, principal, or superintendent)
- higher education administration
- community or local arts organization or arts agency management
- other leadership roles in school/community arts, such as serving on projects, committees, and governing boards
- employment in a music-industry-related profession
- full-time or part-time involvement with other music-related professions
- professional negotiation activities
- mediation and human problem-solving or consulting opportunities

Intellectual

- in-depth expertise and personal resource development in a specific area of music
- expertise in a related field with applications to music
- theoretical or applied research
- articles or other publications to share concerns and ideas
- editorial work to help bring about exchanges of ideas
- methodological innovation
- creative course and curriculum design
- innovative materials development

Musical

- performance in the teacher's major area
- performance in a secondary medium

- recognition of improvisation skills
- recognition through composition skills
- special skills in music theory, music history, or ethnomusicology
- professional leadership through skill in philosophical or sociological applications of music

Instructional

- general or classroom music
- related arts and humanities education
- special music education and music therapy
- preschool and early childhood education
- elementary, preadolescent, or secondary education
- higher education
- evaluation
- technological media and other communication systems

This professional development program is recommended to generate career-long professional effectiveness. Equally important, it is offered as a means of helping retain the best music educators in teaching by providing opportunities for personal rewards, recognition, satisfaction, and advancement.[18] For other professional development ideas, see the Additional Professional Development Suggestions sidebar.

WHAT ARE THE REWARDS OF BEING A MUSIC TEACHER?

The last question that I asked the respondents in my study of professional development was "What are

---

ADDITIONAL PROFESSIONAL DEVELOPMENT SUGGESTIONS

For Teachers

- Be proactive about professional development. Talk with building administrators about your specific needs. Help them understand what you need in order to be more effective with students.
- Work with local music organizations to arrange county and multiple school district in-service programs with other music teachers in neighboring districts.

For State and Local Music Organizations

- Provide opportunities for teachers to share their teaching practices. Music teachers need to talk to other music teachers, and they rarely have the opportunity to do that within their school day.
- Work to get many teachers involved in leadership roles. Executive directors and staff of music organizations must continue to work to get many teachers involved in planning and designing professional development programs.
- Grassroots professional development experiences are usually the most successful. Encourage local-level activities in your organization.
- Move state-level offerings around the state so that teachers in various geographic areas can get to the workshops.
- In your state-level advocacy work, communicate with policy makers about induction, mentoring, and professional development policy for music teachers.

For Music Coordinators/Staff Developers/Administrators

- Value the teacher's voice regarding professional development. Ask teachers what they need and how they want to spend their time. Ask teachers to evaluate programs that are provided to give feedback about their usefulness.
- Arrange for teachers to talk with one another and other music teachers from other districts.

---

the rewards of being a music teacher?" I think it fitting to close the section on "Critical Issues" with some reminders from our colleagues about the rewards of being a music teacher.

Making music. Being an active part in building a community of musicians and learners. I enjoy seeing young men and women develop from goofy freshman to confident seniors. Working with student teachers. (I really feel this is an important part of my job; the reward part has just become a reality as more of my former mentees are becoming teaching colleagues!) (High school instrumental music teacher)

I remember the moment in class weeks ago that Tom found his singing voice, and he has consistently used it since then. I made a big deal out of it in class today, and he was beaming. All through an assembly he kept on catching my eye, smiling, and waving. I think I hooked him. (Elementary general music teacher)

It's easy to recognize all of the injustices of this urban setting that make my job harder than it should be. But, without complaint or resistance, my students do what is necessary to stay involved in the process of learning and making music. Any student motivated by such attributes is a pleasure to teach. I feel there is no better job than one that begins every day with a hug from a child. Regardless of what happens throughout the day, I am the luckiest person in the world to have a job where every day starts like that. (Middle school instrumental music teacher)

I had two girls that were so shy that they refused to speak to adults, often wouldn't even speak to kids, and wouldn't even pick up or touch the materials (bean bag, scarf, rhythm sticks, etc.) to use them, or even hand them back at the end of the lesson. I was really shocked when the first girl sang alone for me and even more shocked when she did it a second and third time. But it meant more to me when the second girl came around because it showed me that the first one wasn't a fluke. I had created a classroom atmosphere that was so comfortable that these girls were able to do things that they couldn't do any-where else. I knew that I was at least doing a little bit of what I had come there to do. (Elementary music teacher)

I find it very rewarding just to make a positive difference in each kid's day. I know that on some days, my class is the only time that some of my students feel successful, valued, or accepted. It is so rewarding for me to see their smiles, hear their enthusiasm for music, and to help them realize just how much they can accomplish. (Middle and high school string teacher)

I feel that there are constant rewards with my job. I feel rewarded when a student is able to identify meter or keep a consistent beat when they were not able to before. I feel rewarded when students express that they had a great time and can show me that they've learned from what we have been experiencing in class through answering questions or giving their own opinion about what we accomplished or interacting with the music through singing, playing their instruments, or moving. I feel emotionally rewarded and rejuvenated every day. I feel rewarded when one or more of my autistic students focus on the musical activity we are doing or sing back a portion of a song we once sang in music or even are able to sit through an activity without throwing the tantrum that they usually do. I feel rewarded when I am able to talk to another teacher about one of their students and we realize that music is a place where that student feels successful even though they are struggling to get by at most other subjects. I feel rewarded when students "get" a musical concept or are able to sing tunes in tune or are able to play something they once thought was tough. It's rewarding when a student finally uses his/her singing voice. It's rewarding to see the students succeed and develop a love for music. I feel successful when they are successful. I've developed a strong pride in my students that is directly connected to myself and it is easy to feel rewarded on a regular basis. (Elementary general music teacher)

NOTES

1. Michael V. Smith and Paul Haack, "The Long View of Lifelong Learning," *Music Educators Journal* 87, no. 3 (2000): 28–33.

2. Harry Price and Evelyn Orman, "MENC 2000 National Biennial In-Service Conference: A Content Analysis," *Journal of Research in Music Education* 49, no. 3 (2001): 227–33.

3. Jim Anderson and Brent Wilson, "Professional Development and Change Communities," *Music Educators Journal* 83, no. 2 (1996): 38–42, 50; Chelcy Bowles, "The Self-Expressed Professional Development Needs of Music Educators," *Update: Applications of Research in Music Education* 21, no.1 (2003): 24–28; Smith and Haack, The Long View of Lifelong Learning"; Brent Wilson and Blanche Rubin, "A Cross Site Evaluation of Getty Center Professional Development Programs" (Manuscript written for the Getty Foundation, 1995).

4. Mary R. Hookey, "Professional Development," in *The New Handbook of Research on Music Teaching and Learning* (New York: Oxford University Press, 2002), 898.

5. Lisa DeLorenzo, "Perceived Problems of Beginning Music Teachers," *Bulletin of the Council for Research in Music Education,* no. 113 (1992): 9–25.

6. Patti J. Krueger, "Becoming a Music Teacher: Challenges of the First Year," *Dialogue in Instrumental Music* 20, no. 2 (1996): 88–104.

7. Bowles, "The Self-Expressed Professional Development Needs of Music Educators," 25.

8. Ibid.

9. Smith and Haack, "The Long View of Lifelong Learning."

10. Price and Orman, "MENC 2000 National Biennial In-Service Conference," 232.

11. MENC staff, written communication, June 5, 2003.

12. The NBPTS standards for music teachers, developed by NBPTS and a committee of music educators, are posted on the Web at http://www.nbpts.org.

13. "National Board for Professional Teaching Standards (NBPTS) Guidelines for Ethical Candidate Support," retrieved July 9, 2003, from http://www.nbpts.org/pdf/policy_ethical_cand_supp.pdf.

14. Ibid.

15. For information on NBPTS research, see http://www.nbpts.org/research/index.cfm.

16. "About NBPTS/State and Local Support and Incentives," retrieved July 9, 2003, from http://www.nbpts.org/about/state.cfm.

17. This section is reprinted, with permission, from Music Educators National Conference, *Music Teacher Education: Partnership and Process* (Reston, VA: Author, 1987), 41–46.

18. Reprinted section ends here.

Colleen M. Conway is assistant professor of music education at the University of Michigan School of Music.

PART V:
LISTENING TO MUSIC TEACHERS

The five teachers who wrote the stories in this part were given no specific directions other than to write a short essay that captured some of their beginning music teacher experiences. It is interesting to note that all five teachers address the beginning music teacher issues that have been documented in research (explored in Part I of this book). The first story, for example, includes references to communicating the value of music education to colleagues or administration, motivating students, being left out of decision making, inadequate materials, isolation, and curriculum concerns, all of which were discussed in Part I.

Colleen M. Conway

"Oh, Didn't They Tell You?"

This first story was written by a recent music education graduate when she was in her second month of teaching. Although the teaching context in this story is unique and the teacher was not working full time, based on my work with many other beginning music teachers in full-time positions, I believe that the issues faced by the teacher in this setting are not unique. Many music teachers start their careers in schools that have had struggling music programs.

"Oh, they didn't tell you?" asks the custodian, as I try to understand the implications of the phrases "moving your furniture" and "art show." "No," I say, still trying to figure it all out as we both survey my classroom. I knew there was an art show happening the next week. What I hadn't known was that it was going to be in my room, that it had always been in my room, and that it was to be set up five days before the event itself. Apparently, the fact that I had classes to teach for three of those days was not a large consideration.

"Oh, they didn't tell you?" and "Oh, by the way ... " are quickly becoming my least favorite phrases to hear at school. I usually have just enough time to freeze my face in a neutral expression and fleetingly wonder what important "detail" I'm about to be surprised by after two months. Past revelations have concerned scheduling (what I was told versus what is actually done), grading (whether students who do not complete any assignments can fail band), and the financial state of my program, among others. While there are certain questions I know to ask, it never occurred to me that I needed to inquire where the art show was going to be held. And getting the information is only a start. There is no guarantee it will remain current, and if not, it is probable I will find out in another "Oh, by the way ... " moment. In many instances, the new information challenges my beliefs about my role as the band director and significantly alters my classroom plans. This near constant shifting and the situations that cause and result from it have been challenging to work through. After two months on the job, I've come to see these conditions as the result of conflicting expectations fostered by a lack of communication.

I believe this lack of communication stems from the unusual position I currently hold and the time of year I started teaching. A month after graduating in December with a bachelor of music in music education, I became the band director of an after-school program. Run by a public school district, it serves students of nearby private schools too small to have their own bands. I had some serious concerns when I accepted the position, but as a December graduate I had few choices, and it was important to me to work as a music teacher, so in January I became the fourth band director in nine months.

Because I began when I did, I was finishing my degree in the fall when all of the staff introductions and new teacher orientations were occurring. The building procedures I learned were for the schools where I student-taught. I keep in contact with my cooperating teachers but have never met the people who were instructing my students in the fall. And even though I'm now in the building, I'm a near invisible teacher because of my atypical hours.

This isolation means that conflicting expectations among the various people involved in my program—students, parents, administrators, and myself—not only exist but can remain hidden. While I consider my job a class (an impression formed during my interview) and try to run it as such, doing so is a challenge because others think of band as an activity, somehow analogous to karate and ceramics! And although I don't know for certain, I believe the previous teachers viewed band as an activity as well. Without the benefit of a summer vacation to put space between my standards for the class and the beliefs of the previous teachers, I am finding the already difficult process of changing perceptions highly challenging.

I'm convinced the difficult situations I've had to work through would be less serious or nonexistent if band was thought of as a class. Parents do not routinely pull their kids out of class ten minutes early for no reason. I think students, if they thought band was more than an activity, would come on a more regular basis, and maybe then I would no longer have days when half the class is absent. I believe they'd practice and take their assignments to do so seriously if their schools demonstrated a commitment to music education by putting band grades on students' report cards. If my teaching was respected for what it is—teaching—I don't think the administration would continue each week to try to add high school students to my fourth- through eighth-grade band to boost numbers. There would not be a prevailing belief that any student can start playing an instrument at any time during the school year. I would have a budget and be able to access the bank account. It is okay to buy instruments for an activity from eBay, but I doubt this is where the textbooks come from!

More frustrating still is the double standard that allows the administration to hold me to the highest expectations while not supporting my standards for my students. I am expected to function as an experienced teacher, regardless of the fact that I began teaching only a few months ago and have not had the support of the school community. I was expected to jump in and fix the program's many problems—a task requiring professional training—and to do it in time for the state aid count. Then I was told that to expect students to come to each rehearsal is unrealistic, as is expecting them to practice, and that it is unthinkable that anyone could get a "U" (for "unsatisfactory") in band!

I have been very fortunate through all of the unexpected complications and twists of my new job to be supported by a caring group of family, friends, and teachers. They've helped me gain perspective, offered advice, and sometimes just listened, and in doing so have greatly reduced my sense of isolation. Perhaps most importantly, they've laughed with me and have more than replaced the support I expected to receive from the school community.

The very day that I began to put these thoughts on paper, I was explicitly told by my building administrator that I might be happier if I thought of my job as an activity. The conversation was surprising as it occurred but in retrospect only confirmed my suspicions about the way my job is thought of by others. Even after this discussion, I am grateful to have this job, which is making me a better teacher and a stronger person. I am resolved to do my best while I am in this situation and look forward to beginning a more traditional job as a slightly experienced first-year teacher in the fall. And while of course there is no guarantee that the art show at my next school will not be held in my room, I will at least know to ask!

Searching for Diversity

In addition to documenting the well-researched topic of beginning teacher isolation, this story addresses some of the less-talked-about but equally evident and problematic issues of diversity faced by beginning teachers.

Twenty-five miles from my liberal, colorful college town lies the small village where I work. Students who go to the middle school here are bussed in from all over, many from nearby cities and many more from the local subdivisions. In seventh and eighth grades, the two grades I teach, there are more than eight hundred students, nearly two hundred of them in band. You could call the area rural, except that most of the land is not devoted to crops but to developments. Still, kids out here are in Scouts and 4-H; they train horses and on Halloween they get their chills in a corn maze. Not too far away is the Ku Klux Klan headquarters for this state. What is a young lefty band teacher to do?

When I first arrived, I had to understand what is important in this community. Three things, mainly: family, family, and family. People move here specifically to raise kids. They move from my college town and from many other more exciting places because here they believe their kids will be safe and well educated. To make sure that happens, parents here are highly involved with school life, some to the point of being overbearing.

Secondly, I had to figure out my place. I was clearly different from most people here: more politically liberal, more familiar with other cultures, Jewish in this vastly Christian town. Suddenly, my morning commute took me to a place where staunch conservatism was the norm, and there were three black children in a school of eight hundred. Oh, and four or five Asian-Americans. This was to be the job where other teachers kindly told me I should go speak to Mr. B., because he was the other Jewish teacher in the district.

There are many things we are not supposed to talk about here. Even the health teachers are prohibited from saying things related to sex that parents find morally objectionable, regardless of whether the information will help students lead healthier lives. And it seems that all of us, no matter what subject we teach, are barred or at least discouraged from treading on the toes of the most conservative set of ideas I have yet encountered in daily life.

I have grown almost accustomed to all this. I haven't gotten used to the sea of white faces and blond hair, but it doesn't jar me the way it used to. I now feel comfortable telling my students that I don't celebrate Christmas or Easter, and that while the Christian tradition has given us a lot of beautiful music, it is important also to seek out and perform music from other traditions. But there are still some old habits of thought that rankle and some issues about who I am and what I believe that people here do not accept. I observed a particularly nasty prejudice during my first semester of teaching.

We all hear kids making fun of each other. We would never accept any blatantly racist epithets or any comments having to do with a person's religion. But there are two words that adults routinely ignore and that kids persist in using, to the detriment of their peers and the community at large. Ready? The words, which you've probably guessed by now, are faggot and retard.

The second word was hard to endure. Every time we came to the end of a piece, I would say, "Watch my baton for the ritard." The snickering would begin, and the two or three special education students in the class would look at the floor. Each time, I calmly explained that "ritard" is a musical term for slowing down, whereas "*re*tard" is a rude name for a mentally disabled person. Then we would rehearse the last four bars of the piece. After a few months, there was no more snickering and no more comments about that word.

Faggot was harder. Many times, hoping to avoid a teacher's scrutiny, a student will use the word "gay" in such a pejorative way that he or she is basically calling someone a faggot without using the specific word. This is my rationale for why I don't let kids use the word "gay" as a slur in my hearing. Okay, maybe the ulterior reason is that I am too close to my one gay relative to let the remarks go by, since I hear them as a personal affront to him. But my motive is not important; the point is that gay is something people are, and not a bad thing, which is exactly what I tell the kids. I let them know that using the word to mean stupid or uncool is like saying someone is stupid or uncool for being another race or religion and is just as offensive. I have made this speech a few times, sometimes to one student privately. Once I had to make it to a whole class.

I heard the word fly across the room just before rehearsal began. I don't know who said it, but everyone heard it. I made the speech. I added, too, that there were probably some gay students in the school, maybe not yet aware that they were gay, and maybe just starting to feel that they might be. I asked the students to put themselves in the shoes of those kids and realize how they would be hurt by the misuse of a little three-letter word. I paused for reactions.

"But I was just saying that he's happy," said the boy who now admitted to shouting it out. While I doubted the truthfulness of this statement, I allowed that it was fine to use the word "gay" to mean happy or carefree. I also explained that the word was not bad in itself; saying someone is gay is not a slur unless you use it as one. A tricky idea, but one with which middle schoolers are already familiar from their daily parlance.

The students accepted my soapboxing calmly. One came up to me after class to thank me for what I had said. By the end of the day, the rumor had started that I was a lesbian. (This was concurrent with the rumor that I was dating the young male teacher across the hall.) Since I don't make it a practice to address rumors about myself, I never said what was on my mind: if standing up against homophobia makes me a lesbian, would standing up against racism make me black? I didn't bother because my work, I thought, had already been done. I had stuck up for the minority. A couple of days passed without incident.

My principal came to see me in my office during a planning period. He is a thoughtful man, prone to quick speech and clear-cut decisions. I can never tell from his face whether the news is good or bad. This time he took a seat and began, "I got an anonymous letter from a parent. I also got a phone call ... ."

There was at least one parent out there, if the call and the letter came from the same person, who thought that I was telling the kids to be gay, that I was promoting homosexuality over and above heterosexuality, that I was trying to influence the students' orientation. I explained to my principal what I had really said, and he not only believed me but also conveyed his wholehearted support. He said that his policy was not to accept anonymous phone calls and that he had thrown the letter in the trash. The news was not all good, though.

"I would be careful what you say," he warned me. Not for his sake, but for mine. He reminded me of where we were, politically. I got the message: speak your beliefs as long as they don't conflict with anyone else's, or risk losing your job.

I don't regret a word of what I said, and I'm not scared of conservatism in its uglier forms. I'm too new at this to be scared. I'd rather protect the students, who deserve to go to school in a safe, caring environment, than protect my own reputation among other adults. Maybe if I lived in this town it would be different. But I can say, after teaching here for a year and a half, that many of my students' parents have become my friends, and they quietly support my activism. It just takes time for the supporters of diversity to come out of the woodwork ... or the closet.

Glad to Have My Mentor

The teacher in this essay had student-taught in the school district where she was hired. In the months before taking her first position, she had been substitute teaching alongside the previous band director who had injured her hand and needed assistance. Her mentor was an experienced band director who had been teaching in the district for a long time. He was well-respected by the music education profession. The school paid and trained the mentor teachers. At the outset of the school year, I believed this teacher was "set" to be successful.

However, here is a sample of comments from this teacher's journal in the early weeks of her first year of teaching.

Is overwhelmedness a word? It is now 6:00 and I just got home. I hate the fact that my planning period is second hour ... (8-27-00)

I wonder if it is normal to feel conflicted about a job like this at the end of the day. On the one hand, it is a great feeling to be getting to know and connecting with these kids. On the other hand, I'm completely exhausted. (8-31-00)

I swear I am on an emotional roller coaster with this job. Yesterday I was in tears thinking I just want out now and never teach again. Today, I just don't know. (9-11-00)

I don't think it would matter if I made twice the money I am making now ... I don't want to work these hours. I have discovered what attracted me to teaching in the first place, but unfortunately it's a minuscule part of my whole job. I'm just tired. (9-20-00)

I guess it would be a waste of my education and ability if I quit at the end of this year ... almost like giving up. However, I'm SURE that this job does not fit with the kind of life I want to have. I guess this is a good way for me to figure out my priorities. (10-1-00)

I hate being like this. I normally can find the positive in my life no matter what is going on, but that's getting more difficult. Especially on Sunday nights ... . I absolutely dread going back. (10-22-00)

Now just completing her third year of teaching, this teacher is able to reflect back on that first year.

Over the past few years I have been working hard at streamlining my job. This includes putting procedures into place for classroom management, paperwork, grading, and other such details. Now that I have a new baby, I am increasingly glad that I have put effort into this and will continue to try to find ways of making my job easier and, more importantly, less time-consuming.

Fortunately, the enjoyable parts of the job are now in better balance with the negative aspects for me.

The next section of this essay is devoted to this teacher's reflection on the role of her mentoring experience in helping her to understand and enjoy her job.

I consider myself to be very fortunate in the mentoring experience I've had as a beginning teacher. I landed a middle school band job in the district where I did my student teaching. In addition, I had previously taught private lessons in the district's after-school program. When it came time for assigning mentors to mentees, two teachers applied to be my mentor. My principal gave me a choice, and I decided to go with the band director at the other middle school. Not only did we have nearly identical job descriptions, but he also had been one of my cooperating teachers and I had taught lessons in his building. I already had a working relationship with him.

It was incredibly helpful to have a mentor who did essentially the same job I was doing. Most of my questions were about things he had experienced, so he was readily able to guide me when I needed him to. He was also able to remind me when deadlines were coming up for festival applications, dues, etc., because his deadlines were the same. Although he would have helped me in this capacity regardless, it did help that the district trained and paid its mentors a nominal stipend. We were expected to meet for an hour once a month (although we were allowed to count some of our e-mail time). At these meetings, he was able to help me in hands-on ways, such as looking at my festival music and helping me decide if I had over-programmed my eighth graders (I had) and going through the mountains of percussion accessories my predecessor had amassed and helping me decide what was usable and what was not.

Some would argue that there is an inherent problem in not having a mentor within the building. I grant that there were questions that were building-specific that I needed answered. It also would have been nice to have someone in the building who could have come to observe my teaching during his or her planning period. This is where it is necessary to do what is best for yourself, your program, and your students. I spent nearly as much time asking the secretaries and custodians questions as I did my mentor. It can be intimidating being a newcomer to the building, but most of the rest of the staff would like to see you succeed!

Again, I was very fortunate that circumstances turned out as they did for me. I like to think that if things had been different, I would have had the courage to seek assistance wherever I could get it ... from veteran teachers, state organization members, former professors, even my own former band directors. Even when I felt fairly certain about my own decisions, it was always reassuring to be able to bounce them off of someone experienced. I hope that someday I will be able to provide that same assistance to a young teacher.

When asked what has made her continue this far in teaching, this teacher responded:

I've said from the beginning that if I ever end up quitting this job, it won't be because of the students. Maybe the paperwork or the bureaucratic garbage, but definitely not the students. That is the single most important reason I continue to do this job ... I love my students. Making music with them is just like icing on the cake for me. It is a passion I have, but the students have become my foremost inspiration to continue, especially now that I have a baby. If I did not enjoy my job, there is no way I would be returning because there is a big part of me that would like nothing more than to stay home with my daughter. I feel as though my students are all my kids, too, and I don't like the idea of deserting them. I get to do something that none of the other teachers in my building gets to do, and that is to see the same group of kids every school day for three whole years. It's an amazing thing to watch them grow ... musically, of course, but also physically and emotionally. I feel that the rewards outweigh the difficulties.

Not only has this teacher just completed her third year of teaching, but she also continues to develop as a leader in the instrumental music profession. She often communicates with her mentor and other instrumental music professionals about important issues of teaching and learning music. Would she have been successful without her mentor? Would she have continued in the profession? I imagine that she would have continued and been successful. However, when I read her journal and listen to her interviews and get a sense of her true struggle in the early months, I am grateful that she had someone to talk to about her experiences.

Band Festival:
A Competition or a Checkup?

This essay focuses on the high-stress and sometimes high-stakes event of taking an ensemble to band festival. Although stressful for all music teachers, the preparation of an ensemble for an adjudicated festival can be even more difficult for beginning teachers trying to find time for standards-based instruction and assessment in addition to quality performance. This particular teacher was reflective enough to be able to use a negative festival experience as a learning experience.

Band festival is one of the more stressful times of the school year for me. Stressors include parent and community expectations, differing philosophies on festival, past festival experiences, future reputation of the program and, most importantly, the emotional state of the students. The stress can also be connected to the various ways that people view festival and its purposes. Is it a competition? In the eyes of many parents, students, administrators, and teachers, the answer is yes.

I am currently completing my second year at my present school after two years in a previous position, and I frequently hear from colleagues, district directors, and clinicians about how poorly this program has performed in the past. One particular clinician told me that based on how poorly this band had performed over the past years, it will take time for judges and people in our part of the state to believe that this program is heading in the right direction. I am my eighth-grade band students' fourth teacher in three years. I am facing an accumulation of four totally different philosophies, teaching techniques, and personalities, which plays a huge role in how a band performs.

After receiving ratings lower than I had anticipated at festival this year, I was concerned to see how this demoralized the group. Students started to doubt their abilities and hard work. Students and parents started to say how mean and horrible the adjudicators were. I have noticed that some directors feed off that and claim no responsibility for the ratings. It is very easy to let your band and community members blame the festival judges for a poor rating. This year, my band was given a "poor" rating, and I could have taken this road, but I decided to address the problem. I did not listen to the taped performance until the following Monday, with my students. I asked them to really honestly think about what each judge had mentioned. Were their remarks valid? Were they right in saying what they said? I disregarded the ratings and focused on what these clinicians had to say. Ratings, honestly, do not mean that much to me. I look at festival as a musical physical. It is more important to hear what the judges have to say and then make a point to use their suggestions in classroom teaching. I also reflected on my shortcomings as a band director. I know that there are some holes in what I do, and it is apparent in the consistent comments from each clinician.

When I talked to the other music directors in my school about addressing my problems in teaching, they felt that I had lost my teaching "edge," and my spouse was very worried that all of my confidence was gone. I felt quite the contrary. For the first time, I felt confident enough to say that I had a big problem in my musicianship, and I looked for help from other directors and college professors. I also turned my post-festival lesson plans towards more of the fundamentals, as I was advised to do by the clinicians.

Festival participation is vital for a program to grow. It is essential to teach the students in the band program that they are going to hear things from the judges that are not always going to be pleasant, and that is all right! My top group took great offense at being told that they had not performed great, and they were angry. I had to really convince them that these clinicians were looking out for the best interest of the students. I read through those comment sheets over and over throughout the year and remind the students of our shortcomings. Are we still playing too loud? Is our group balanced? Can we play softly enough to hear if we are in tune with each other? These are all questions that we need to ask our band members on an everyday basis.

Is festival a competition? As I started my teaching career, I firmly thought that the answer was a definite yes, but now I have felt my answer evolve to a solid no! I do believe that a festival can become a competition if the director allows it to be perceived that way. If I feel as though I am competing against any other band, I put the blame on myself. The "pressure" of ratings is something that can be avoided if you educate students, parents, administrators, and colleagues about the benefits of getting priceless feedback from experienced clinicians. The judges are not heartless and cruel people who want to destroy programs; they are usually band directors who are able to give feedback and advice to bands and their directors on how to have more successful performances and effective rehearsals. Band festival should be considered a yearly medical checkup. Outside listeners can hear and see things that will maintain the health of the program, if the directors are eager and willing to make necessary changes. Band festival is not a competition, but it is an event that can make or break a program, a teacher's career, and the students' enjoyment and success.

No Teacher Left Behind

This essay provides a fitting end to this book, as it offers both positive and negative examples from the teacher's experience. It also covers nearly all of the beginning teacher issues documented in research, including communicating the value of music education to colleagues and administrators, developing rules that facilitate effective classroom management, motivating students, student discipline, physical exhaustion, isolation, poor equipment/facilities, and curriculum concerns. It should be noted that this teacher just completed her third year of middle school orchestra teaching in a suburban school district that is one of the most well-supported music programs in the state.

I am told that we are in the midst of a national teacher shortage. The baby boomers are retiring, and struggling schools are begging teachers to work. I recently received my *NEAToday* Magazine in the mail and was pleased to see an in-depth article about the *No Child Left Behind Act*. As I read through the countless hoops that I'll have to jump through to continue my career as an educator, I couldn't help asking myself, "Why are we trying so hard to leave teachers behind?"

There is a reason we have a national teacher shortage. Teaching is not easy, nor is it convenient. It can be very frustrating, and the "thank you's" can be few and far between. However, there are great rewards to teaching! There are moments when I smile and realize the impact of my work on the lives of our children and future society. Entering my fourth year of teaching, though, I wonder if the rewards of teaching can begin to balance the discouraging aspects.

Here are some of the negatives and *positives* that I've faced:

Many days, I wake up tired. As I put my key into the door to let myself into my building, the lock jams. I cannot open any of the doors. I walk around to the front of the school. School starts. I spend the first half of my class period helping students tune our school cellos. As often as I try to explain to the custodians and my administrators that the instruments will go severely out of tune and some will crack if we turn the heat off in our building each night, it does not seem to make a difference. Today was not an exception. The fine tuners are bent. The pegs don't fit well. Five cellos have broken strings that we can't afford to replace. "Matt, would you mind trading off your cello throughout the hour with Sam; we don't have enough instruments today." There is no money to fix the instruments. I'll repair what I can during my lunch period.

Fifth-grade orchestra. Ninety-five students crammed into two merged classrooms, with instruments. I am grateful I have a team teacher. While I tune the beginners' instruments, my team teacher runs around the building looking for chairs. We are missing five. A stand falls over due to the fact that it is old and will not remain tight. The stand lands on a student's instrument; it cracks down the middle. "I don't have a stand." "I need music." "I don't know how my bridge fell off—it was like that when I opened the case." I look at the line of forty students waiting to be tuned. I see students trading instruments with each other. I see students racing on top of their music folders like skateboards. I call out to them to sit down; they can't hear me. I decide that we are not tuning today.

[Following our Fall "String Fling," a collage of all our orchestra ensembles, a parent and young viola player approach me. "Chris, is that you?" I exclaim, recognizing a viola player from my first year in the district. "Yeah, it's me– sophomore this year," he grins sheepishly. His mom steps in, saying, "We just wanted to thank you. When Chris first started with you in eighth grade, he was really struggling on the viola. He couldn't read music and he was ready to quit. You really encouraged and helped him learn to love playing again." "Yeah," Chris laughs, "I got good, or something." "Anyway, Chris never would have continued in music if it wasn't for you, and we wanted to thank you."]

Music teachers have an extra burden to share in that they continually have to explain the importance of music education in a child's education.

I started my job with a host of new ideas. Fresh from college, I learned how important it was to "teach the student," not "teach the concert." I felt prepared to open my students' minds to a whole new dimension of music. The problem was that few students understood or were prepared to learn what I had to teach. "Homework?! This is *orchestra*; why do we have to do homework?"

I faced similar comments from parents and the school counselors. "I will pull my child out of class if you require him to practice." "This isn't math class. Students should be allowed to socialize, be a little looser, have more fun." I was fortunate. My school principals supported me. It took a lot of discussion with them about my goals for the students, but eventually they understood and shared my views.

[My current seventh-grade orchestra is made up of the first group of students I started in orchestra upon coming to the district. For three years, I explained to them the importance of singing and hearing a pitch before playing it on their instruments. After three years of acting like a cheerleader to get my students to sing, it paid off. I first noticed it when I saw a violinist in my orchestra turn off her tuner and instead use the A on the piano to tune. She played the A, hummed what she heard, and then played her open A string. She continued listening and humming until she finished tuning all four of her strings. Then she checked her violin with the tuner. I chuckled to myself as I saw her smile after seeing that she did indeed tune accurately without the assistance of her tuner.]

I've mentioned some of the more obvious challenges of teaching, but sometimes the smaller, everyday issues can be equally draining.

It is spring. It is our first five-day week in a month. "Do we have to play today?" "Can we have a free day?" "Can we watch a movie?" Fifteen comments like these in under five minutes. Constant chattering. Constant plucking. Constantly having to explain the importance of professionalism and respect in class. Students constantly rolling their eyes. Poking each other. Coming to class unprepared. Dropping instruments. Having to use the bathroom. At least one person playing one past the cut-off, each time. Complaining, whining, flirting, daydreaming, interrupting, distracting. Between teaching students to be good, polite individuals and disciplining the students who misbehave, I teach music maybe fifteen minutes in a forty-minute class period. They don't prepare you for this in college.

[I love the little unexpected surprises: goose bumps after a good perform-ance. Students bringing me self-compositions. Students repeating phrases I've uttered when coaching each other during a sectional. Hearing an arrangement of "La Bamba" leading into "Wipe Out" leading into "Big John MacNeil" leading into "Mason's Ape-ron." Walking into the orchestra room and seeing "Orchestra Rocks!" written on the board.]

When the good moments happen, they are truly sweet. Why do I continue to teach? Because I am good at teaching. I love music. I truly believe that music education is important. As I said before, teaching is not easy. Do I see myself teaching in ten years? I don't know. I will, however, stick with it for as long as I can because I know that what I do is important.

Appendix:
State Mentoring Initiatives for New Teachers

The information in this section is drawn from responses to a spring 2003 survey by the MENC Information Resources staff. The survey was sent to several leaders in each state, including presidents and managers of state music educator associations (MEAs) and state arts supervisors or department of education representatives. The key question on the survey was, "To your knowledge, does your state have any mentoring programs for new music teachers?" Some states updated the answers given to MENC on a similar survey in spring 2002. Others provided completely new data. All responses have been edited for style and length.

For further information, contact the state MEA, or contact the state music/arts supervisor or a representative in the department of education. This listing also includes Web sites related to some state programs.

ALABAMA
Mentoring is conducted by each separate division of AMEA. The vice president of each district within each MEA division makes the assignments in the district, then reports them to the vice president of the division. Then the assignments are reported to the AMEA vice president for follow-up. This is working well on a regional level in the smaller districts. The state does not have one person to oversee any comprehensive mentoring programs.

ALASKA
Alaska State Mentoring Program Standards were approved by the state board of EED in spring 2003. There is approximately $1 million a year in federal "Retention and Recruitment" dollars flowing through EED to school districts, and many of those efforts focus on mentoring.

Anchorage, Mat-Su, and Fairbanks have mentoring programs for first-year teachers in all disciplines that follow the State Mentoring Program Standards. Other smaller districts have programs that are in their infancy.

On the Web: www.educ.state.ak.us.

ARIZONA

The AMEA established a program at the state level. At the district level, there are a number of formal and informal programs, but they are not coordinated through AMEA.

ARKANSAS

The Arkansas DOE has implemented the Pathwise Mentoring Program developed by Education Testing Service.

On the Web: http://arkedu.state.ar.us/teachers/index.html#mentoring.

CALIFORNIA

The state program, BITSE, is funded partially by districts, which adds a local support requirement to the process. It is a program for all first- and some second-year teachers and is not specific to music teachers. It is advertised, especially to teaching graduate students. Most people using the program work with a peer teacher within their school. In the last few years, the state MEA has taken a more active role in structuring sessions specifically for new teachers at the state music education conferences.

COLORADO

While some districts do encourage and organize mentoring programs for music teachers, other districts, especially small ones, do not. CMEA and the general music council sponsored a special session called SAFE (Support a Future Music Educator) during the MEA conference. The objective was to bring more new teachers and college students into the sessions at the conference. Various activities were planned for communication and discussion between new and veteran teachers. The effort lasted about two years. Each chair-elect of the general music council determined the activities.

CONNECTICUT

By statute, all new teachers who have not had three consecutive years of teaching experience in another state are required to complete the Beginning Educator Support and Training (BEST) program. During this initial certification period, they receive help from a mentor assigned to them by their school district. In most cases, beginning music teachers are assigned a mentor who is a music educator. Regardless, mentors must be trained and must be given released time to assist their assigned beginning teacher.

On the Web: www.csde.state.ct.us/public/der/t-a/index.htm.

DELAWARE

Mentoring is handled at the district level with state support; more and more districts are participating. Delaware has nineteen school districts that range in size from very small (a high school and middle school with one music educator each) to large metro-politan districts. Mentoring occurs if there is an abundance of music teachers and if there is a perceived need for it.

Delaware Mentoring Council Web site: www.delawarementoring.org.
University of Delaware e-mail address: info@delawarementoring.org.

DISTRICT OF COLUMBIA

The District of Columbia has an informal program in place. Currently, the DC Department of Education is working with the Professional Development Department to develop a more formal and comprehensive approach.

FLORIDA

Florida is committed to assisting individual teachers and school districts. A major focus of FMEA's strategic plan is on developing a comprehensive mentoring program for new teachers, teachers new to Florida, and experienced teachers in need of assistance.

On the Web: www.flmusiced.org.

GEORGIA

Teachers who are new to teaching with less than three years of experience are eligible to apply for an assigned mentor. The program is also available to teachers who are new to the state of Georgia, regardless of their teaching experience. These teachers must complete an application requesting a mentor. All mentor-mentee assignments are made by the state chair for a period of two years. Mentors also must complete an application to be considered for an assignment.

HAWAII

At this time, the state MEA has no program for new teachers. The state averages three to five new music teachers a year—total—and has a very tight-knit community. There is much informal support available for teachers in Hawaii. Word travels fast about any problems, large or small.

IDAHO

There is no statewide program, but many districts assign mentors to new teachers. Many rural areas assign mentors outside of the mentee's discipline who function as "sounding boards." Contact the IMEA for more information.

ILLINOIS

Illinois has a voluntary program for beginning music teachers. The MEA makes its presence known through mailings, the MEA journal, and announcements at district events. The MEA mentor chair put together a booklet titled "How to Survive as a Beginning Teacher." At state conferences, a breakfast is served to all first- and second-year teachers. A mentor sits at a table with four or five young teachers, and they have a conversation. New and experienced teachers from the breakfast keep in touch all year via e-mail.

INDIANA

In Indiana, the Department of Education requires all new teachers to be assigned a mentor within the school or district. There is a semiformal training session for new teachers and their mentors that is sponsored by the IDOE and several regional education service centers. IMEA also holds an annual first- and second-year teacher workshop designed to address the specific challenges faced by new music teachers. This program features an initial training session and a midyear follow-up session.

IOWA

The beginning teacher mentoring and induction program was created by Iowa Legislature in 2001 and is administered by the Iowa DOE. Required of all public school districts in the state, it promotes excellence in teaching, enhances student achievement, builds a supportive environment within school districts, increases the retention of promising beginning teachers, and promotes the personal and professional well-being of classroom teachers.

On the Web: www.state.ia.us/educate (click on TEACHER QUALITY/Induction Resources).

There is also a program run jointly by the IMEA and the Iowa Choral Director's Association. According to the program brochure, "Music Mentors of Iowa is dedicated to providing trained mentors in all areas of music education. We work to develop positive, professional relationships among mentees, experienced teachers, administrators, and faculty/students in teacher education programs."

On the Web: www.icdamusic.org/mentor/mentor-brochure.pdf.

KANSAS

KMEA started to investigate statewide mentoring in spring of 2002; the statewide program completed its first year in May 2003. It targets music teachers in the first three years of teaching. This past year, the MEA compiled a list of experienced teachers (with at least five years of experience) who are willing to become mentors. Twenty-eight new teachers have been placed with a mentor. The project focuses on pairing mentors and mentees who are near each other geographically so that there can be personal contact, as well as phone calls, e-mails, etc. The MEA believes a personal relationship between a mentor and mentee is necessary for the best results. The program encourages teachers to exchange classroom visits.

KENTUCKY

The Kentucky MEA does not have any established mentoring guidelines. However, the Kentucky Department of Education has a Kentucky Teacher Internship Program (KTIP), which all first-year teachers are required to pass in order to receive provisional certification. The "10 Kentucky New Teacher Standards" provide the framework for the internship program. The internship committee is composed of a mentor (a teacher in the system), the administrator, and a teacher educator (a college/university representative).

LOUISIANA

Louisiana requires all first-year teachers to have a mentor for two years until the new teacher passes the Louisiana Teacher Assistance and Assessment Program. If the new teacher does not pass the LTAAP in the first two years, he or she must complete a two-year professional development program. Then he or she starts the two-year process again with a mentor teacher. If the new teacher does not pass the LTAAP following this last two-year period, he or she may not teach in the state again. This is a state-sponsored initiative for all subjects. The LMEA does not have any additional programs or requirements.

MAINE

Maine is just starting a mentoring program. The state is also working on the certification process review. The MMEA has tried mentoring on a district level. District III has had a mentor chair and program for several years. Other districts have conducted informal activities. The experienced teachers in the state are willing to help.

MARYLAND

The MEA, not the state department of education, coordinates a statewide mentoring program. First- and second-year music teachers throughout the state are paired with mentors. The program is three years old. It's not large, but it has been helpful to many new music teachers.

MASSACHUSETTS

There is no statewide program for mentoring new music teachers. Each city or town in the Commonwealth has its own system; quality varies. Budget cuts are affecting music programs statewide.

MICHIGAN

The state now requires new teachers to be paired with a mentor for the first three years. They are given time to meet, and the mentor is paid a stipend. However, new music teachers can be paired with another music teacher or an experienced teacher in another subject who teaches in the mentee's building. For more information, contact the MMEA or the Michigan Department of Education.

MINNESOTA

Many local districts offer formal mentoring programs, but this is done on a district-by-district basis. At the state level, there is no formal program. The MMEA does invite beginning teachers to the state conference for a half-day workshop, a "mentoring morning." The workshop draws only a small portion of the state's newer music educators (between fifteen and thirty), but it seems to be productive. Minnesota Educators of the Year and some select board members are invited to help facilitate the discussion. There is some opportunity for follow-up after the meeting, but it is not a formal mentoring program.

MISSISSIPPI

The junior high and high school MEA divisions assign mentors to new teachers in the state. The mentor (a local teacher) is responsible for keeping the new teacher informed of current developments and policies in the state governing high school activities, assisting in preparing for competitions, giving advice on programming, etc. In many cases, elementary music teachers offer assistance at the local and district levels on an informal basis. Elementary music teachers are assigned mentors at the local (school district) level.

Some local school districts provide meeting time for music teachers at the beginning of the school year. This provides a time for the new teachers to be welcomed and meet a teacher who will be his or her mentor for the year. The fall elementary MEA division workshops (in September) are the first district meetings to offer support, information, and professional development for both new and returning teachers.

Formal mentoring guidelines will be offered by the state MEA at the state MEA convention in 2004 to districts that do not yet have an established mentoring program. Additionally, teachers seeking National Board Certification (through the National Board for Professional Teaching Standards program) are assigned mentors through the local school districts where they teach or through the university that is offering the NBPTS course. The teachers who serve as mentors are all national board certified and volunteer their time.

MISSOURI

The MMEA has established a mentoring program throughout the state of Missouri. A well-qualified group of music educators representing all levels and areas of music education are available to provide help, advice, or just listen to a teacher new to teaching or new to the state. Many of the larger school districts in the state have their own mentoring system. MMEA mentoring is geared more toward small school districts where specialized mentoring is not available. Contact the MMEA for further information.

MONTANA

Montana has district-level programs only, initiated by individual districts. There is no statewide or MEA mentoring program.

NEBRASKA

The Music Mentor Program (MMP) was created by the NMEA and the Nebraska Council on Music Teacher Education (NCMTE). The program is designed to help music educators and administrators deal with music classroom issues. The program brings together experienced music educators with first- or second-year teachers who request assistance with any aspect of their music program.

NMEA Web site: www.unl.edu/NMEA.

The brochure is available at: www.unl.edu/NMEA/nmea.html#mentor.

NEVADA

Currently, Nevada's mentoring programs are at the district level only. However, as the NMEA continues to develop its strategic plan, the association will work to define mentoring and develop a statewide program.

NEW HAMPSHIRE

New Hampshire recognizes the importance of mentoring programs in attracting and retaining quality educators in all disciplines. To this end, in 2002, the New Hampshire State Department of Education established a mentoring task force to design statewide guidelines to assist local districts in developing their own mentoring programs. This is not a statewide mandate; local districts will be responsible for establishing their own programs.

Additionally, New Hampshire provides mentoring for new teachers through some of its alternative certification routes. The state's Alternative IV certification is available to content areas that fall into a critical shortage category, such as music, which has been on the critical shortage list in New Hampshire for several years. In this program, the Superintendent of Schools or designee works with the individual and a certified mentor in developing an Individual Professional Development plan leading to full certification. The candidate has up to three years to complete the plan.

NEW JERSEY

New Jersey has a new mentoring program in place that varies from district to district. Once prospective candidates pass the Praxis exam, they are issued a certificate of eligibility to pursue a teaching position. When a contract is granted, the district provides a mentoring support team consisting of the principal, the content area supervisor, and a colleague teacher.

NEW MEXICO

The NMMEA supports a volunteer program. New teachers, teachers in new positions, and principals are made aware that the program is available through contact with association members and direct mail. If a new teacher or principal wishes to use the program, he or she is assigned to work with a retired music educator. For more information, contact the NMMEA.

NEW YORK

The state of New York has a mentoring program for all new teachers, including music teachers. According to the NYDOE, all new teachers in the state should have mentors. Mentoring programs are run and funded at the local level. The effectiveness of these district programs varies.

For further information, see the NYDOE Office of Teaching Initiatives Web site: http://unix32.nysed.gov:9220/tcert/resteachers/mentorinternship.htm.

NORTH CAROLINA

There is a formal state mentoring requirement for all teachers without public school teaching experience. It is monitored through the state department of public instruction. Mentors are paid a stipend of $100 a month for their first two years of mentoring. Music teachers are not necessarily placed with a teacher in the music field, but they are placed with an experienced teacher. The NCMEA has two programs that try to place new music teachers with experienced music teachers. Also, some districts try to match music teachers with other music teachers in their district.

NORTH DAKOTA

North Dakota has a mentoring program for music teachers in the state. A handbook with a lot of useful information for new teachers was distributed at the NDMEA annual meeting last year to teachers around the state. The North Dakota state education department is also working on a statewide mentoring program, and several larger cities have mentoring programs within their districts to service new teachers. The NDMEA tries to match up mentors and new teachers based on area of specialty and geographic location.

OHIO

Ohio has a mentoring requirement for all new teachers and a program in place to support the mentoring process. Each new teacher is assigned a mentor within the district. That mentor is responsible for assisting the new teacher in any way and even helping prepare the teacher to pass the Praxis 3, which is the third part of a test required to become certified in Ohio. There is no money from the state to fund this process, and it is therefore completely up to the school districts to provide competent mentors.

OKLAHOMA

The OMEA invites all first-year music teachers to its annual convention. The conference registration fee for first-year teachers is waived. A luncheon is held in honor of the first-year teachers. Each new teacher receives a booklet that contains names, addresses, and phone numbers of the OMEA executive board, as well as resources, helpful hints, and copies of articles on relevant topics for new teachers, including rules and regulations, recruiting, contests, rehearsing, lessons, budgets, music advocacy, and encouragement. There is also a state-sponsored mentoring program. Contact the Oklahoma University Department of Education for more details.

OREGON

The OMEA has an informal mentoring program that has been in place for about three years. It is advertised in MEA journals. Upon receiving a request from an active or new music teacher, the OMEA tries to find a retired teacher in the requestor's geographic area to serve as a mentor. Though the program hasn't been heavily used, reports have been very positive. The MEA emphasizes that the program is open to anybody, and that requesting a mentor is not an indication that the requestor is in trouble or performing poorly.

PENNSYLVANIA

Mentoring programs exist at the local level in all 501 school districts. The programs are district-initiated, not state-sponsored.

RHODE ISLAND

There is a mentoring program through the Rhode Island Department of Education. However, music teachers are not necessarily paired with music teacher mentors. The RIMEA has spent part of this past year working on a mentoring program for music teachers. This would be offered to various school districts to augment their current mentoring programs. The RIMEA hopes to have a pilot program in effect by summer of 2003 for the fall semester.

SOUTH CAROLINA

The SCMEA strategic plan has a mentoring component, and several MEA divisions have mentoring plans in place. The Band division has an especially strong program. At the SCMEA conference, a couple of special sessions were offered, and a drop-in period was held with the SCMEA president and officers to acquaint new teachers and prospective teachers with the profession, as well as with the workings of the SCMEA and its links to the SCDOE.

SOUTH DAKOTA

One SDMEA goal for 2003–04 is to develop a mentoring program for music teachers in the state. It would be an MEA-sponsored initiative, not a state-sponsored one.

TENNESSEE

Tennessee has mentoring programs in many locations at the regional level. Programs are voluntary and use retired members as mentors. The TMEA is currently promoting such a program statewide.

TEXAS

The TMEA has implemented the TMEA mentoring network. The State of Texas also has a mentoring program—Texas Beginning Educator Support System (TxBESS)—but it is for teachers of all disciplines.

Web site: www.tmea.org (click on mentoring network).

UTAH

A state-level initiative was in the works until funds dried up. The only state-level efforts are happening through the UMEA. District-level mentoring programs for new teachers are not discipline-specific programs. The UMEA program welcomes new music teachers by providing them with a copy of the UMEA teachers' directory, important forms, contact information for specific questions they may have, and an MENC membership form. Still under development is a plan to assign each new teacher with a mentor from UMEA—someone the new teacher can call, e-mail, meet with, etc.

VERMONT

Vermont requires every school district to have a mentoring program in place for all beginning teachers, as of September of 2002. All teachers are required to have mentors during their first two years of employment.

VIRGINIA

Virginia has district-level mentoring. The VMEA is looking into starting a statewide program as part of its strategic plan.

WASHINGTON

Washington has a state-sponsored program. The WMEA as a whole does not have a program; there are twenty-two MEA districts in Washington, each with its own president and officers. There are mentors for new music teachers, but it varies from district to district. Typically, the Union is responsible for arranging for a music teacher mentor for a new music teacher. Mentor teachers are paid to assist new teachers. The state provides funding for mentoring to districts.

WEST VIRGINIA

The WVMEA does not have a mentoring program but is considering starting one. Some local school systems have informal programs. Individual schools around the state have mentoring systems in place to help their new teachers.

WISCONSIN

The state is starting a program for all new teachers, to be implemented in 2004. The WMEA is also developing a program that may be on-line before 2004.

WYOMING

2003 is the third year of Wyoming's mentoring program. Every summer the WMEA sends a mailing to all principals and superintendents in the state. The WMEA requests information on new music teachers in the various districts. The WMEA then contacts these new music teachers and invites them for a two-day mentoring session in Casper. The WMEA pays all expenses for the new teachers. The new teachers are introduced to people from various parts of the state that represent music teachers, principals, the music industry, the WMEA, the WEA, and the activities associations. Each organization explains its role in education and lets the new teachers know about the services available to them. Then the WMEA introduces new teachers to their volunteer music mentor who teaches in their district. The MEA also assigns the new teachers to a mentor who works in their building to help them with the day-to-day business of school. The WMEA contacts these new teachers about once a month for encouragement and to find out how they are doing.